THE
HOME
WORKPLACE

Compiled by the editors of Organic Gardening and Farming* Magazine

Table of Contents

Introduction

Inventive, thrifty, resourceful, self-reliant: the qualities that mark the competent home craftsman have much in common with those we attach to successful gardeners and farmers.

Of course, there's a strong economic incentive for doing your own building and repairs around the homestead—the same incentive as for home canning and saving energy in the home—but even beyond the money saved and the superior workmanship, there's the special satisfaction that comes from being in daily contact with the fruit of your own labors, be it a homemade tool shed, compost bin or simple gate latch. You probably could have bought one as good, but it would never take on the special meaning of its handmade counterpart.

Then too, there are many valuable tools and structures that are simply not available commercially—that one must either build for oneself or do without. Many of the structures and devices of traditional, low-technology farming and homesteading fall into this category. Smokehouses, for instance, and springhouses. Cold frames, solar driers, grape arbors, cisterns, hay sweeps, dairy goat and cow stanchions, woodlot sheds and countless hand appliances for garden and orchard that could never be mass-produced at a profit: nothing fancy, these devices and techniques are examples of what is now being called appropriate technology, low-impact technology or post-industrial technology. They're good for what they're good for; they get the job done.

Portable Cold Frame

Here's a highly practical cold frame with the distinct advantage of portability. Place the unit in an east-west alignment to start earliest plants right in the garden, then move the cold frame down the row for later-starters. The device is also handy for seeds started in flats, and will keep many vegetables going strong late into the winter. Hinged windows permit easy ventilation.

Fall is a good time to use a cold frame to prolong your supply of head lettuce, celery, Swiss chard, endive and parsley. When nights get very cold, cover the frame with a blanket and bank leaves around the sides.

Construction

1. Measure 6 inches up along one side of the plywood, as illustrated. At this point, mark a 45-degree angle and draw a line the height of the window sash. Repeat on the other side of the plywood.
2. Cut out the two plywood end-pieces to exactly the same size.
3. Measure the width of your window, multiply by two, and add ¼ inch.
4. Cut two pieces of 1x6 and one piece of 2x4 to the proper length.
5. Cut four gluing blocks 1½x1½x6 out of the leftover 2x4 and assemble.
6. Attach window sashes to the 2x4 spine with hinges.
7. From the remaining 1x6, cut four pieces 2 inches wide by 15 inches long for handles. Round off 5 inches on one end of each handle and fasten to the sides with 6 p. nails and glue. Sand lightly and paint.

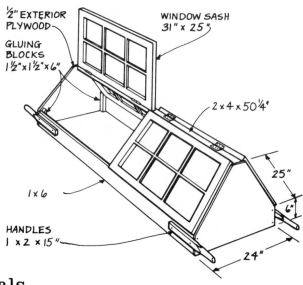

Materials

Four used window sashes, approximately 31"x25". (Size of windows used can vary, but avoid windows so large that the finished unit will be difficult to move.)

  1 piece 2"x4"x8'
  2 pieces 1"x6"x8'
  1 piece ½" exterior plywood, 77"x24"
  6 p. nails
  1¼" finishing nails
  4 pairs hinges

Non-Tip Sawhorse

A pair of good sawhorses is an essential component of every workshop. This particular style has the advantage of not tipping over when you stand on the ends. Another practical feature is that all but one of the saw cuts required in its construction are made at the same angle.

Construction

1. Cut the 6-foot piece of 2x6 in half. Set the saw at an 18-degree angle and rip (cut *with* the grain) the ends of the two 2x6's to a length of 66¾ inches, as illustrated.
2. At the ends of the 6¾-inch cuts, cut complex angles on the 2x6.
3. Cut eight 22-inch legs from the 2x4. Cut both ends of the legs at a complex angle of 18 degrees.
4. Cut four end braces from the 1x6. Rip the top and bottom of each piece to an angle of 18 degrees.
5. Assemble by nailing the crosspieces to the legs, then nail on the end braces.

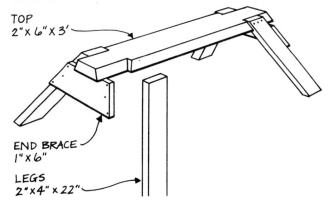

TOP
2"x 6"x 3'

END BRACE
1"x 6"

LEGS
2"x4" x 22"

Materials

> 1 piece 2"x6" (6 ft.)
> 2 pieces 2"x4" (8 ft.)
> 1 piece 1"x6" (44")
> 24-8 p. nails
> 24-6 p. nails

Wheelbarrow

Every gardener needs a good wheelbarrow. The wheelbarrow is one of those perfect tools, highly functional, beautiful in its simplicity, incapable of being "improved."

Construction

1. Cut out of hardwood two pieces 2x2x58 for handles. Using a drawknife, wood rasp or block plane, round off 8 inches on one end of each handle. Finish with sandpaper.
2. Cut out remaining hardwood pieces: two pieces 2x2x14½ for legs, four pieces 1¾x1¼x24 (three for supports between handles, one for top of front of wheelbarrow) and four pieces 1¾x¾x13 for side supports.
3. Lay out the handles as shown. Scribe marks on handles at each intersection of supports and also at bottoms of support pieces. This will give the proper angles for mortise and tenon cuts. Cut handles and supports ⅝-inch deep, as shown.
4. *Wheel assembly.* From 1x12 white pine stock, cut six pieces 20 inches long. Cut one piece of ¾-inch flatiron 11 inches long. Drill two holes 9½ inches apart to accommodate nail used to scribe circle.

Place two 20x1x12 pieces side by side and scribe circle with the flatiron. To avoid weakness caused by the wheel's center hub falling at the point where the two pieces of wood join, drive a 6 p. nail 1½ inches in from the edge of the center of the boards. Put the other nail in the outside hole of the flatiron and scribe another circle. Remove the nails and cut out the circle with a jigsaw. Use these two pieces as patterns for the other four. Glue the pieces together, using C clamps and #10 1½-inch wood screws. Glue the pattern pieces with the center mark last to facilitate drilling the 1-inch center hole for the axle. Bend a 61½-inch piece of 1¼-inch flatiron around the wheel and secure with six 1½-inch #10 wood screws.

5. Using a hand drill or drill press, drill a ¾-inch hole in the wheel end of the handles, making sure to get the proper angle for the ¾-inch axle. Using a 1½-inch #10 wood screw at each joint, assemble the handles and support pieces. Cut the legs as shown, and assemble them in front of the first support piece using ⅜x4 carriage bolts.

Assemble the wheel as shown, using a 22x¾ piece of threaded rod, four nuts, four flat washers and a piece of 1x2¼ pipe.

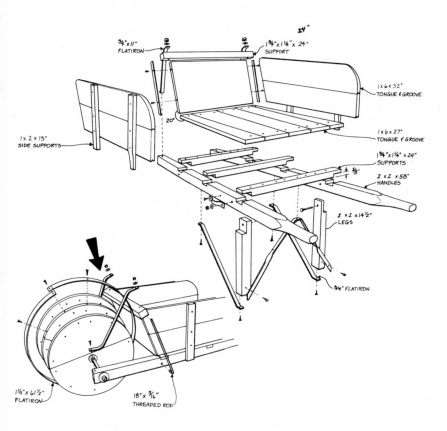

Have all materials on hand before beginning construction. Wooden wheel is made of three layers of 1-inch stock glued and secured with ten 1½-inch wood screws on each side.

6. From 6-inch roofers (tongue-and-groove boards) cut five 27-inch pieces. Lay on support braces as illustrated. Fasten each board to the front and rear support braces with 1-inch #10 wood screws. Trim off the excess.

7. Install the ¾-inch flatiron support braces on the legs as shown, using a vise to bend the angles. Fasten with 1½-inch #10 wood screws.

8. *Assembly of front piece.* Using one piece 1x12x19 and one piece 1¾x1¼x22, assemble as illustrated at a 20° angle. Plane the front of the bed to achieve a good fit. In the 22-inch top piece, drill two ⁵⁄₁₆-inch holes on 20⅞-inch centers, ⅜ inch from inside edge. Cut a second piece of ¾x11 flatiron, use it, along with the identical piece you cut and used for the compass, as a brace between top piece and front of handle shaft. Fasten to the shaft with 1½-inch wood screws. Cut in half a 36-inch piece of ⁵⁄₁₆-inch threaded rod. Drill holes in the handle and bend the bottom of the threaded rod (approx. 1 inch) so that it fits securely in the hole. Repeat for other side, then tighten at the top with nuts, as illustrated.

9. *Assembly of side pieces.* Cut four pieces of 1x6x32 tongue-and-groove board and two 6-inch pieces of the ¾-inch flatiron for the side brackets. Place two of the 1x6's in the opening between the front piece and the threaded rod; tap boards forward until they are flush with the back edge of the bed. Mark boards so they are flush with the front piece, then trim off the excess. Drill a ⅜-inch hole on the rear side of the flatiron bracket and a hole for a #10 wood screw on the forward side. Fasten the brackets to the sides, as shown. Fasten the two 1¾x¾x13 braces to the sides with 1-inch #10 wood screws. Round off the corners of the sides with a jigsaw, as illustrated. Sand lightly and apply the finish of your choice.

Materials

5 pieces-¹⁄₁₆"x¾"x36" flatiron
1 piece-⁵⁄₁₆" all thread (36")
1 piece-¾" all thread (22")
4-⁵⁄₁₆" nuts
4-¾" nuts
4-¾" i.d. flat washers
2-⁵⁄₁₆" i.d. flat washers
2 pieces 1"x6"x12' tongue-and-groove roofers
1 piece 2"x7"x8' hardwood
1 piece 1"x12"x12' white pine (#2 common)
28-1½" #10 wood screws
40-1" #10 wood screws
2-⅜"x4" carriage bolts
1-2¼"x1" galvanized pipe

Row Maker

Once your seedbed is tilled and raked, you can save the trouble of lining out individual planting rows with a simple row maker. The pegs are removable for wider rows.

Construction

1. Rip a 6-foot piece of knot-free 2x4 or 2x3 to 1½ inches square, and round off 4 feet of one end with block plane, drawknife or wood rasp until it's comfortable to the hand. Then rip a 3-foot piece of 1x6 into one piece 2 inches wide and two pieces ¾-inch wide. Sand all edges until smooth.

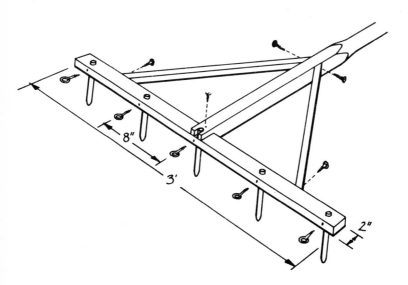

2. Cut a notch ¾-inch wide and 2 inches deep in the bottom of the handle. Remove wood with coping saw or wood chisel.
3. Starting 2 inches from either end of the 1x2x36 piece, drill five ¾-inch holes on 8-inch centers, 1 inch from outside edge. Also drill five holes large enough to insert #5 screw eyes to act as stops for the dowels.
4. Insert the 1x2x36 piece into the notched end of the handle. Apply glue to the notched end of the handle and insert into it the 1x2x36 piece. Fasten with a 1-inch #10 wood screw. Lay the two ¾x¾x36 pieces as illustrated, mark the angles, saw and fasten each end with glue and a 1-inch #10 wood screw.
5. Saw a ¾-inch dowel into five 6-inch pieces. Round one end of each. Insert the pieces into the ¾-inch holes and turn in the screw eyes. A light coat of linseed oil helps preserve the finished row maker.

Materials

1 pc. ¾ dowel (30")
1 pc. 1½x1½ (6')
1 pc. 1"x6"x36"
5 screw eyes #5 galvanized
5-1" #10 wood screws

Straight Row Marker

Construction

Cut a ¾x36 dowel in half and sharpen one end. Sand both ends lightly. Then drill a ¼-inch hole 1 inch from the top of each dowel and mount a cleat to one stick so the string may be wrapped to prevent tangling.

Materials

1 pc. ¾ dowel (36")
1 pc. 1" white pine (7"x2")
2 #10 wood screws

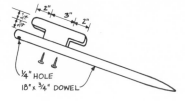

2" 3" 2"

¼" HOLE
18" x ¾" DOWEL

Soil Sifter

A simple sifter for compost or potting soil can be made by nailing a piece of ¼-inch hardware cloth to the bottom of a 12x8 frame.

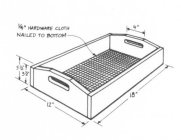

¼" HARDWARE CLOTH
NAILED TO BOTTOM

4"

5½"
3½"

18"

12"

15

Easy-to-Build Insect Traps

As any organic gardener will tell you, a garden is supposed to be a place of peaceful coexistence between plants, insects and man. What to do, then, when the bugs fail to get the message and start laying claim to more than their share? There are, of course, dozens of natural sprays, dusts, rotations and other remedies for crawling, chewing and sucking pests in the garden, but one of the best ways of dealing with winged insects is to catch them in flight.

Featured on the following pages are the imaginative responses of three gardeners to their insect problems. The first two traps use light as an attractant; the third is a box-trap design intended primarily for greenheads and horseflies. All are easily constructed with a basic assortment of hand tools.

Dick's Bug Machine

When Gladys Geddes of Winsted, Connecticut, again ventured into raising chickens after a 25-year vacation from them, the high price of feed soon led her to look for ways to include less costly protein in their diet. Her husband Dick suggested insects, but collecting the quantity needed seemed more outrageous than the cost of commercial feed. So he devised a machine that, although it's really just collecting them, sometimes seems to be manufacturing insects.

In brief, the machine works this way: flying insects, attracted to a light, are sucked through a fan located next to the light, and are exhausted into a collection bag. Dick Geddes used materials he had on hand, so the machine cost him nothing. The fan is the biggest expense, and if you don't have one kicking around—and you probably don't—scout out a used or surplus one, since a new model will be expensive. The remaining materials are commonplace. Geddes used wood scraps, a peanut can, and a nylon stocking.

The nice thing about Dick's Bug Machine is that it doesn't really produce bugs and insects. It actually depletes the insect population. Mrs. Geddes noticed a marked reduction of green cabbageworms in her garden after the machine went into use. In fact, she had prodded her husband into making several more of the devices, not to produce more chicken feed, but to protect her garden plants.

The Bug Machine is operated at night, being turned on at sunset and off at dawn. The overnight collection is usually sufficient for the poultry.

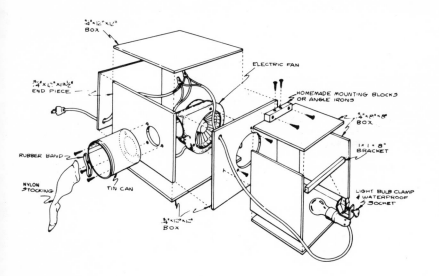

Construction

1. From ¾-inch plywood, cut four 12-inch square pieces and a piece 12 inches by 13½ inches. Nail the square pieces together, forming an open-ended box, using 6d nails.
2. Measure the diameter of the fan intake and cut a hole that size in the center of one side of the box. Mount the fan in the box, intake against the hole cut for it, exhaust directed out one of the open ends of the box.
3. Place the remaining piece of plywood against the open end through which the fan exhausts. Mark the location and size of

the exhaust on the plywood, then remove the plywood and cut out the exhaust hole. Cut a similar-sized hole in the bottom of the peanut can and secure it over the exhaust hole with three ½-inch #6 screws. Finally, nail the plywood to the box, using 6d nails.

4. Cut four 8-inch-square pieces of ¾-inch plywood. Nail them together, forming another open-ended box. Cut an 8-inch length of 1x1. Nail it across one open end of this box, so the light socket can be clamped to it, with the bulb inside the box.
5. Secure the light box to the fan box, using small corner irons or a homemade mounting, as shown in the photo.
6. Slip a nylon stocking over the exhaust pipe and secure it with a stout rubber band.
7. Plug in the light and fan. A 40-watt bulb will provide adequate light.

Materials

Wood
    1-2'x4' sht. ¾" ext. plywood or
        Sides: 4 pcs. 12" sq.
        End: 1 pc. 12"x13½"
        Sides: 4 pcs. 8" sq.
    1 pc. 1x1x2' or
        Brace: 1 pc. 1x1x8"
        Mounting block: 1 pc. 1x1x4"

Hardware
    6d nails
    3-½" #6 screws
    1 light bulb clamp and waterproof socket
    1-40-watt light bulb
    4-1" #6 screws

Miscellaneous
    1 electric fan, approx. 4½" intake
    1 tin can
    1 nylon stocking
    1 heavy rubber band

Pennsylvania-Style Trap

Another bug catcher that's inexpensive and easy to build is what inventor Andy Merkowsky calls his Pennsylvania-style trap. It can be built largely with scraps, but even if all materials are bought it is more economical than commercial models. Like Dick's Bug Machine, this model operates on the principle that insects are attracted by light. The bug is attracted and, in attempting to fly around the light, flies into a baffle and is knocked down. Where the Bug Machine uses a plain 40-watt bulb, however, this design calls for a 15-watt fluorescent black light, attached vertically. Another difference is that this model is designed to be hung from a post or tree.

Like the Geddeses, Merkowsky puts his captured insects to good use. He feeds fish with them, either by floating the trap directly over the pond or by suspending it out over the water from the shore. Of course, it's just as effective right in the garden, positioned at a height of five or six feet. The black light is turned on at night, when flying insects are most active. Fish are quick to respond to being fed daily at a given place and time, says Merkowsky, and different species have definite culinary preferences, with bluegills selecting the mosquitoes and smaller bugs, and catfish and bass opting for the moths and larger catch.

Merkowsky recommends the trap be constructed in the following sequence.

Construction

1. Start by cutting four pieces of ¼-inch exterior plywood 6 inches by 19 inches. These will be used for the baffles.
2. The next step is to cut frame and lampholder supports. Using ¾-inch white pine, rip four pieces 15¼ inches long and 1⅜ inches wide and cut a ¼-inch by ½-inch-deep dado lengthwise down the exact center of all four pieces.

3. Cut cross-lap joints at the center of each of the four pieces. Glue the pieces together to form two X's.
4. Apply glue to the ¼-inch grooves and insert the baffles into the cross frames. Paint the unit a flat black.

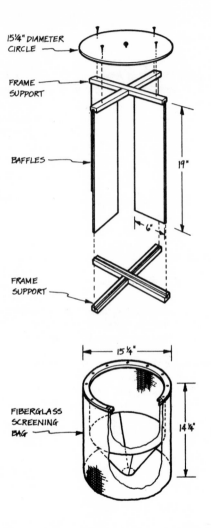

5. When the paint has finally dried, position and glue the lampholders onto top and bottom cross supports with an epoxy or other waterproof glue. Be sure the lampholders are placed so that the bulb will be in the exact center of the baffles.
6. Cut two 15¼-inch-diameter circles from ½-inch exterior plywood. Cut out the interior of one circle to leave a 1-inch

thick ring. Paint both pieces flat black. Using 1-inch #10 wood screws, attach the solid circle to the top of the baffle supports and the 1-inch ring to the bottom. Fasten a screw eye to the center of the top for hanging.

7. Fashion a holding bag from fiberglass screening. Cut a rectangular piece 14¼ inches by 44 inches. Attach this piece to the outside perimeter of the ring with thumbtacks, and sew the ends together. Then cut a circular piece 16¼ inches in diameter and sew to the bottom. Fasten a 9¾-inch by 43-inch rectangular piece to the inside of the ring. Finally, to make the funnel through which the insects will fall, cut a 9-inch by 9-inch by 6-inch isosceles triangular pattern from cardboard. Starting 1¾ inches from the seam, place the pattern on the bottom edge, and remove four triangles, leaving 2½ inches between. Sew up the adjacent edges to form a funnel with a 2-inch opening at the bottom.

Materials

Wood

1-15¼″ diameter circle, ½″ ext. plywood
1-15¼″ od, 13¼″ id ring, ½″ ext. plywood
4-15¼″x1⅜″x¾″ white pine
4-6″x19″x¼″ ext. plywood

Hardware

6 ft. of 24″ fiberglass screen
8-1″ #10 wood screws
1-18″ black light, starter and holder unit
1 plug and screw eye for top
1 length of elecric cord
flat-black paint

Box Trap Greenheads

The salt marsh greenhead fly, *Tabanus nigrovittatus,* is an abundant and bothersome summertime pest along eastern coastal marshes. Because the female greenhead bites during daylight, and because of its high numbers, long flight range, and persistent attacks, these pests can limit one's enjoyment of gardening, picnics, and other outdoor activities throughout much of the summer.

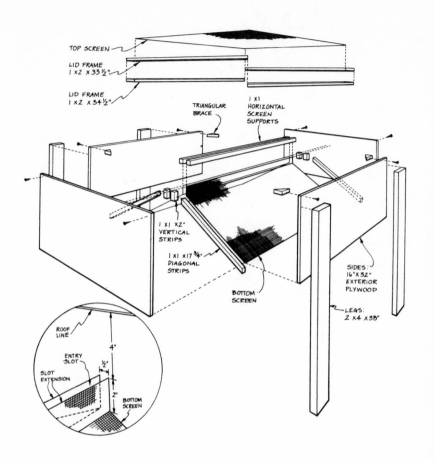

Conventional methods of biting-fly control such as those used for mosquitoes, are either environmentally dangerous or economically impractical. Both adults and larvae of greenhead flies are large by comparison to other, nontarget organisms. In general, the larger the insect, the heavier the dose of insecticide needed to control it.

The box-trap design was tested by Elton J. Hansens of Rutgers University and E. P. Catts of the University of Delaware in East Coast salt marsh areas. Their results indicate that it does capture greenhead flies in sufficient numbers (about 3,000 flies per day) to noticeably decrease the problem. The trap provides an ecologically safe, inexpensive, effective means of control. Traps should be set out during the last week in June and kept operational through August. Maintenance is simple. Tears or holes in the screens or sides should be patched or plugged. Trapped flies usually die in less than 24 hours. Removal of dead flies is unnecessary because they dry and decompose rapidly.

Trap location is quite important; success varies greatly between sites. In general, traps should be placed on the marsh edge near the upland or along the open edge of wooded or shrubby areas. The best locations are at breaks, or openings of low vegetation in screening stands of trees or tall brush near the marsh. Clusters of two or three traps in a fly-path tend to capture more flies than the combined totals of isolated traps.

Vegetation beneath and around the trap should be kept low, four to six inches high, for about a 12-foot radius.

The trap is basically a black, four-sided box on legs, having a screen top and inverted V-shaped bottom. Flies enter the trap from below through an entry slot at the top of the V. The sides of the box can be made of nearly any kind of paneling, including plywood, cardboard, or plastic sheeting tacked to wooden framing.

The trap dimensions have been developed through experimental trial and error, and the builder should try to stick to the 16-inch by 32-inch dimensions—larger and smaller box traps were found to be less efficient. These dimensions allow five sides to be cut from a standard 4x8 panel with minimal waste, which is good to know if you are making more than one trap.

Following the guidelines established by Hansens and Catts, a box trap was constructed in the OGF Workshop. Here's how it was done.

Construction

1. Cut four 16-inch by 32-inch pieces of ½-inch exterior plywood. Form a box frame by butting two end-pieces against two side-pieces and nail it together using 6d nails. Cut two 2-inch-square pieces of 1-inch stock, then cut each in half on a diagonal, producing four triangular braces. Attach one in each corner of the box frame, at the top, using two 1-inch #6 screws.

2. Working inside the frame, locate the vertical center line of the ends. Cut four 2-inch lengths of 1x1 stock. Using 1-inch brads, fasten two inside each end of the frame, locating them, as shown, 4 inches below the top and ½ inch apart, parallel to the center line (one a ¼ inch to each side of the center line). Now measure from each vertical strip to the closest corner, as shown, and cut a strip of 1x1 to fit, mitering the butt ends to ensure a snug fit against the side of the vertical strip and in the frame corner. Each of these strips should be about 17¾ inches long. Fasten in place with 1-inch brads. Finally, measure from vertical strip to vertical strip across the box, and cut two horizontal screen supports from 1x1 and fasten in place, using the 1-inch brads. Each horizontal support should be about 31 inches long.

3. From 2x4 stock, cut four 38-inch legs. Attach them to the trap box, locating them 2 inches shy of the top edge of the box and

positioning them with a broad face against the side of the box and flush with the corners. Drive several 4d nails through the box into each leg.

4. Construct a frame to hold the top screening. Cut two 34½-inch lengths and two 33½-inch lengths of 1x2, making the cuts through the broad face of the stock on a 45-degree angle. Assemble the slightly over-square frame, using mitered corners, with glue and 4d nails.

5. Paint the trap inside and out with glossy black paint.

6. Once the paint has dried, cut metal (not plastic) insect screen to fit and staple it to the bottom edge of the 1x1 supports inside the trap. The screen should extend down the vertical strips and along the descending diagonals to the bottom edge of the frame. The two horizontal braces will hold the screen the proper ½-inch distance apart. Cut screen to fit over the top frame and staple it in place. Then carefully fit this screened lid over the open top of the box trap.

Materials

Wood

1 sht. ½" ext. plywood or
    Sides: 4 pcs. 16"x32"
1 pc. 1x2x12' or
    Corner braces: 2 pcs. 1x2" sq. (cut as indicated)
    Top screen frame: 2 pcs. 1x2x34½"
                        2 pcs. 1x2x33½"
1 pc. 1x1x12' or
    Vertical screen supports: 4 pcs. 1x1x2"
    Side screen supports: 4 pcs. 1x1x17¾"
    Horizontal screen supports: 2 pcs. 1x1x31"
1 pc. 2x4x14' or
    Legs: 4 pcs. 2x4x38"

Hardware

6d nails
8-1" #6 screws
1" brads
4d nails
Glue
Glossy black paint
Staples
1 pc. 36"x84" metal insect screen or
    Bottom: 2 pcs. 32"x20"
    Top: 1 pc. 34½"x33½"

Drip Irrigation the Homemade Way

Drip irrigation uses less water to keep a garden growing in dry times, but the typical cost usually turns people off. Here is a way to build your own system, and save a bundle.

The long, hot summers in southern Texas can cause gigantic watering problems. For Jack Kimberlin, a retired seagoing captain, the answer is a unique homemade drip irrigation system to keep his Corpus Christi garden wet and growing.

He uses only the easiest to handle and most readily available materials. "I never think of buying anything," says Captain Jack. "I just use what I find lying around." The components of his drip system prove it—pins, aluminum tubing, and discarded plastic jugs are at the heart of the 15 or 20 variations of drip irrigation he has in his garden.

Kimberlin says, "With this watering system, there isn't any wasted water. It all goes directly to the roots where the plant needs it. Just enough to stimulate it and keep it growing."

As for the conveniences—Captain Jack sums it up like this, "I fill them up with water once in a while and they do their job day and night whether I'm around or not." Here are three of his systems that typify what homemade drip irrigation is all about:

1. These are the basic parts of this drip system. A wide-mouth plastic jug is best to use because it allows you to get your hand inside to tighten the nut on that side of the hose fitting. If you do use a small-mouth jug, rig up an adjustable wrench to a longer handle and use that to secure the nut inside the bottle as you tighten the hose fitting from the outside.

   The rest of the parts are the same regardless of the jug you use. Pieces of small garden hose, wooden or metal plugs for the ends of the hose, an aeroquip hose fitting, a metal washer and nut to fit the inside of the hose fitting, a rubber grommet, and a cotter pin. This equipment will make one outlet from the container. Any size can be used, but because the volume of water is not of primary importance—it really is a drip system—¼ inch and smaller parts are the best. Often more than one outlet per container is desirable.

2. Cut a hole the size of the hose fitting very close to the bottom of the container. Insert the grommet and hose fitting into the opening.

1

2

3

3. After putting the metal washer on the part of the hose fitting on the inside of the jug, use your hand or a wrench to hold the nut as you turn and tighten it into place. This connection will eliminate any wasteful leaks.
4. After jamming the hose over the outside portion of the hose fitting, stop up the end of the hose with a wooden or metal plug.
5. About one inch from the end of the hose, make a small slit and insert the cotter pin. The pin can be opened and closed to regulate the flow of water, and it keeps the opening from clogging.

4

5

6

6. Punch holes in the top of the lid or place screening over the opening, especially on small-mouth jars, to allow air to enter the container. Remember more than one hose outlet is often preferable.

A variation of this same irrigation system that will supply water to a whole row of crops is just as simple to construct.

The water container in this case should be larger; 25- or 50-gallon drum is best. After putting the hose fitting into the drum—use the same method as with the smaller plastic jug—a simple on/off valve can be added, to allow control over the amount of water released to the crops during any one-watering period.

Attach a two-hose connector to the on/off valve and place the lengths of hose onto the connector and run them down the row of crops. By attaching the hose to a wire or pole just off the ground the hose will remain free of soil and prevent the clogging of the drip points. At each plant insert a cotter pin into the hose about six inches on each side of the plant and a steady supply of water will nourish your plants while you tend to other gardening chores.

Joseph Amici of Orlando, Florida, has devised yet another variation of a can drip system that aids his plants in the hot, sandy soil of this southern state.

What you need to construct this system is a used 1½-gallon paint bucket, small pieces of ¼-inch rigid vinyl tubing (this depends on how many outlets you want), a number of feet of ¼-inch flexible vinyl tubing, cut into a desired length for each of the outlets, wooden or metal plugs for the tube ends and window screen.

Drill holes into the sides of the bucket—four to six seems to be the ideal number. Insert the rigid 1-inch pieces of vinyl tubing into these holes—they should make a tight fit. Copper tubing can be a good substitute for the vinyl tubing.

Now force the flexible vinyl tubing or a small diameter rubber hose over the tubing. It's important that each of the pieces of tubing or hose you attach to a single can are the same length. If they vary in length, the amount of water delivered to the plants will also vary.

Stop up the ends of the tubes or hoses with wooden plugs and poke holes in the hose—if you want to make the water come slowly from drip holes. Always make the same number of holes in each outlet. If you want a more rapid flow just allow the water to come out the unimpeded end of hose.

Next, cut a large hole in the paint can top and fit a cover of window screen over it. Attach by punching holes in remaining ring of metal and threading extra wire through holes to secure the screen. This will allow air to enter but will keep leaves and twigs out.

An important thing to remember is if you plug up one of the outlets, you should plug up all the others from that can in order to equalize the pressure and allow an equal flow to each plant.

If you can't find what you need to make one of these proven systems, use what you've got, and while keeping the principles that make these work in mind, put your own system together.

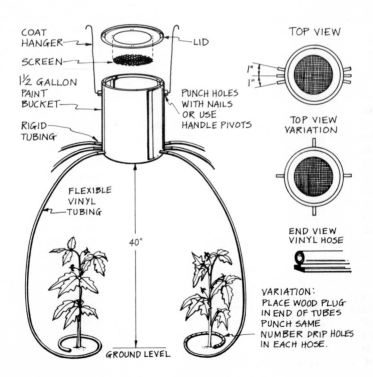

COAT HANGER
LID
SCREEN
1½ GALLON PAINT BUCKET
RIGID TUBING
PUNCH HOLES WITH NAILS OR USE HANDLE PIVOTS
FLEXIBLE VINYL TUBING
40"
GROUND LEVEL

TOP VIEW

1"
1"

TOP VIEW VARIATION

END VIEW VINYL HOSE

VARIATION:
PLACE WOOD PLUG IN END OF TUBES PUNCH SAME NUMBER DRIP HOLES IN EACH HOSE.

Drip Irrigation for Your Garden

We live and garden in west Texas where the average rainfall is 14 to 18 inches, most of it coming in July and August, our "rainy season." Since the frost-free season extends from mid-April to mid-October, some type of irrigation is essential. Our first garden was watered via a combination of irrigation ditches and a sprinkler hose, but neither of these methods was really adequate. For any but small gardens, they are time-consuming and wasteful of water.

This past year we tried a new way of watering our large garden—drip irrigation. It proved to be a sound choice, greatly reducing our time spent watering and practically eliminating evaporative water loss. Freed from watering chores, we planted and produced more vegetables than we would have otherwise.

The basic components of drip irrigation are polyethylene hoses and emitters. Shaped like tiny hollow arrow points, the emitters are inserted at regular intervals in the hoses. When watering is done slowly for a long period of time, a bell-shaped moisture pattern forms beneath each emitter as the ground becomes saturated. This deep moisture insures good root development. We were amazed at how far this moisture spreads laterally—one can dig halfway between any two rows and find moisture at a depth of four to six inches. The fellow who first designed drip irrigation is said to have been inspired by a leaky outdoor faucet, where he noticed plants grew better when supplied with a constant though small amount of water daily.

Our garden consisted of 24 one-hundred-foot rows spaced 4½ feet apart. A ½-inch polyethylene pipe was placed down the length of each row and emitters were inserted at 18-inch intervals. The emitters control the water flow so that pressure is constant throughout the line. Plastic plugs were inserted into one end of each dripline, and the head of the dripline was connected to a ¾-inch polyethylene "header" pipe. The "header" was in turn joined to a garden hose running from a water faucet (see diagram).

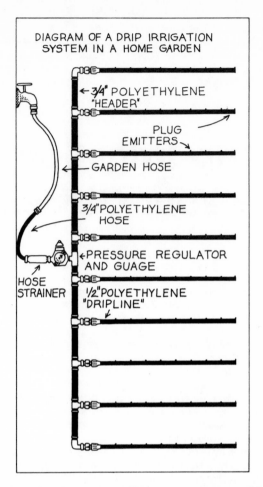

DIAGRAM OF A DRIP IRRIGATION
SYSTEM IN A HOME GARDEN

← 3/4" POLYETHYLENE
"HEADER"

PLUG
EMITTERS

GARDEN HOSE

3/4" POLYETHYLENE
HOSE

← PRESSURE REGULATOR
AND GUAGE

HOSE
STRAINER

1/2" POLYETHYLENE
"DRIPLINE"

By turning the water faucet on all the way, we were able to water six rows simultaneously, opening the valves on the six rows to be watered and closing the others. These same six rows were watered for four hours at a time before rotating to six different rows. During the dry season it was necessary to irrigate every third or fourth day, and in the case of newly planted seed, a group of six rows might be irrigated through the night.

No technical expertise is required to install a drip system. The only special tool needed is a modified pair of needle-nose pliers, used for snapping the emitters into place. Once set up, the system is fairly maintenance-free.

We did experience minor problems with clogged emitters. Generally, these resulted from heavy rains that somehow washed sand into the system. We were able to clear some of the emitters by pulling them out of the pipe and blowing the sand out. Others had to be placed in boiling water before the sand particles worked loose.

Planting commenced as soon as the lines and emitters were in place. Row crops, whether plants or seeds, were planted as near to the driplines as possible. Double-row cropping with a row a few inches from each side of the line was also very successful. Squash and other cucurbits were planted in hills around every third emitter in a dripline.

Driplines may be placed above ground, as ours was, or buried if a more permanent location is desired. Buried hoses are said to last longer than hoses left exposed to the weather, but we've had no experience with them and remain skeptical of their efficiency. For the gardener who tills or otherwise turns the soil, it seems necessary to place lines above ground. We laid mulch (spoiled hay and used paper feed sacks) right over the driplines. The mulch was invaluable, both for conserving moisture, and for keeping down the weeds which thrive as much on the drip system as do the vegetables.

Accessories available for use with this system include an automatic timer for turning the water on or off and a liquid fertilizer injector. We're considering integrating the injector into our system—it would be an ideal way to utilize fish emulsion.

What about expenses? Here is a breakdown of ours (circa 1976):

108' of ¾" polyethylene pipe @ 8¢/ft.	$ 8.64
2400' of ½" polyethylene pipe @ 7¢/ft.	168.00
2000 emitters @ $87.50/1,000	175.00
1 pressure regulator with gauge	17.50
24 plugs @ 40¢ ea.	9.60
24 plastic valves (three broke) @ $1.50 ea.	36.00
3-½" metal gate valves @ $4 ea.	12.00
24-¾"x¾"x½" combination tees @ 45¢ ea.	10.80
1 strainer	5.25
24 female hose couplings @ 75¢ ea.	18.00
24-½"x¾" hose adapters @ 50¢ ea.	12.00
3-¾" insert male adapters @ 40¢ ea.	1.20
1 insert tool	7.50
48-¾" clamps @ 45¢ ea.	21.60
	$503.09

Optional items are the automatic timers ($127.50) and the liquid fertilizer injector ($72.50).

Is the drip system worth its cost? We didn't keep records of our yields, but we canned over 200 quarts of vegetables, filled a 15-cubic-foot freezer, and sold $500 worth of excess produce. In our case, the system practically paid for itself in the first year of operation.

Drip irrigation is especially suited to the arid and semiarid Southwest, but it could be effectively used by virtually any gardener who irrigates extensively. For those gardeners who must pay for their water, it seems particularly attractive.

Tom and Carol Hodges

Do-It-Yourself Garden Cart

Looking at my old, worn-out garden cart and scared off by the price of the new ones, I decided to build one especially suited to my own needs.

The two shortcomings of my previous cart were its small wheels and limited load capacity. My solution to the first problem was easy—two 20-inch bicycle wheels and front forks. The 1.75-inch tires with these wheels are adequate, but 2.25-inch tires would be better still in the garden. For an axle, I welded a 30-inch piece of ½-inch water pipe between the two forks, just above the axle slots. (The length of this pipe determines the width of the cart body.) A ⅛-inch-by-2-inch-by-4-inch steel plate was then welded to the inside, near the top of each fork. The pipe is then attached to the bottom of the cart with two pipe clamps, using four ¼-inch round-head bolts with lock nuts and cut off flush. The two plates are drilled and two ¼-inch round-head bolts are used to attach the forks securely to the body of the cart.

I wanted the box to be as large as possible without causing the wheels to buckle. The dimensions I decided on are 29 inches by 36 inches for the bottom and 29 inches by 48 inches for the top, with a height of 18 inches. All wood is ½-inch exterior plywood. All edges are glued with waterproof glue and nailed with 2-inch galvanized nails. Each corner is reinforced with ⅛-inch aluminum or steel plate attached with ¼-inch round-head bolts and lock nuts.

The axle assembly, attached to the body as described, is designed to permit the angled front to lie flush with the ground when the cart is tilted forward. The skids are made by bending electrical conduit to shape, then attaching them to the body so that the cart sits slightly nose up. The handle (48 inches long and 30 inches wide) is bent from thinwall conduit. It could also be made from two pieces of 1-inch-by-2-inch-by-48-inch hardwood, drilled and fitted with a sturdy broom handle or water pipe and bolted firmly to the sides of the body.

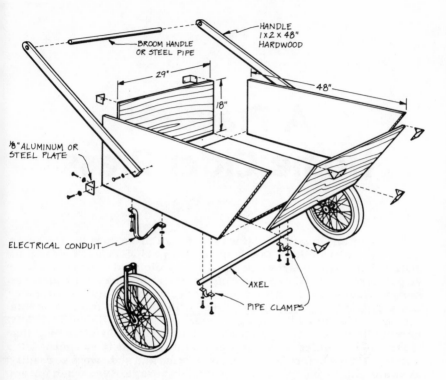

HANDLE
1 x 2 x 48"
HARDWOOD

BROOM HANDLE
OR STEEL PIPE

29"

18"

48"

⅛" ALUMINUM OR
STEEL PLATE

ELECTRICAL CONDUIT

AXEL

PIPE CLAMPS

All parts, both metal and wood, get a coat of primer, followed by two coats of epoxy paint. The bottom of the cart is protected from abuse with a piece of plywood or sheet metal, cut to size and placed in the bottom when necessary. To haul pine straw and other light but bulky materials, I made up some 18-inch-high slat sides that fit into brackets for easy installation.

Donald E. Pierce

A Practical Home Cider Press

Not too many years ago, it was standard procedure for the home apple grower to take a few bushels of his NORTHERN SPIES or JONATHANS to a nearby cider mill. In a while, he'd return home with an oak barrel full of the best-tasting natural apple cider you could ever hope to whet your whistle on. As cider grew in popularity, the cider mills got busier, forcing families, who wouldn't think of going through the winter without a good stock of apples in the cellar, to buy or build their own little fruit presses. During the cold winter months, most of these apples would be pressed into cider as it was needed.

In those days before coffee, tea, fruit juice and soda were so readily available, apple cider was our national beverage. Even when it went bad, it did so in such a delightful way.

The juice press we constructed at the OGF Workshop is modeled closely on a plan developed by the Canadian Department of Agriculture. The unit is designed primarily for apples but can be used for pressing any pulped fruit free of large stones. With apples, the press can handle from one to five boxes at a time, yielding up to ten gallons of juice per pressing.

The essential parts of the press include the frame, drainboard, rack, trays, platform, grater and hopper. It is best to construct the parts in the following sequence:

Frame—Parts I, T, L and C

The four corner posts (I) are made of dressed 4x4, 47 inches long. (Dressed size will vary from 3½ to 3¾ inches). These posts are joined together with 2x4 braces (T), placed 12 inches from the bottom, and across the top. These are set into the corner posts so that their outer surface is flush with the piece ¾x2½ inches nailed to the posts immediately above the lower braces. The 28-inch-long 2x4 braces and the 28-inch pieces of ¾x2½ are cut at 45-degree angles at the corners.

The top 2x4 braces (T) on both sides of the press are strengthened by 1½-inch angle iron (C) 19¾ inches long. Holes large enough for ½-inch rods are drilled 9⅜ inches (measured to the center of the hole) from each end of the 2x4's. Two pieces of 1½-inch angle iron 19¾ inches long, with similar holes 5⅜ inches from each end, reinforce the lower side braces (T). Bore holes in the 2x4 braces to correspond with the holes in the angle iron. The ½x37-inch rods (L) are put in place, and the nuts tightened until the rods are firm.

The same 2x4's in the lower group that are drilled to accommodate the ½-inch rods are also notched in four places to take care of the reinforcements on the rack (P). Cut the notches 1½ inches wide, 1¾ inches deep, and ⅜ inch into the 2x4. Cut two of these notches ⅛ inch in from the corner post, and the near side of the other two notches 6 inches from the corner post.

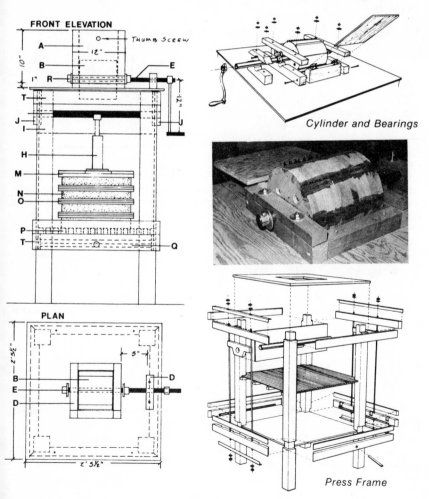

Cylinder and Bearings

Press Frame

35

Drainboard—Part Q

Cut a piece of ½-inch plywood so that it fits tightly into the square space formed by the lower 2x4's (T). Place the plywood so that its high side opposite the drain hole is 2 inches below the top of the 2x4 brace, while the side near the outlet hole is 2½ inches below the top of the 2x4. Any rough stripping can be used to form a ledge for the ½-inch plywood, while small right-angled triangles of ¾-inch material can be nailed in the corners for reinforcement. To make a molding for the top side to seal the joint between the plywood, the braces, and the corner posts, plane ½x⅜-inch strips to almost a triangle in cross section. The drainboard catches the juice and delivers it to the 1-inch hole in the 2x4 brace in the front of the press.

Rack—Part P

The rack is made of 19 pieces of 1x1 nailed onto four stringers of 1¼x1⅞ inches. The stringers are spaced so that they will fit into the notches in the side braces. The stringers and the 1x1 pieces should be made of oak, as the rack has to withstand the full pressure of the jack. To allow room for the corner posts, cut off the two 1x1 pieces on each side of the rack flush with the first stringer. The rack is removable to facilitate cleaning.

Lath Trays—Part O

Each tray requires 14 pieces of ⅜x1½x19-inch lath, placed parallel to one another and the thickness of a lath apart. These laths are crossed at each end (above and below) with laths that hold the rack together. Copper clout nails, one to a lath, are driven in from both sides. Up to five trays can be used at a time.

Pressure Platform—Part M

The pressure platform is made of three pieces 1x6x19-inch crossed by three identical pieces. This platform is subjected to considerable strain, so be sure to nail it thoroughly with nails long enough to clinch.

Bearing Assembly for Grater Supports— Part G

Take two pieces of 2x4, each 12½ inches long, and rip to 2¾ inches. In the middle of these two pieces (6¼ inches) drill a 1-inch hole, 1 inch in from the edge. Rip the 12½-inch pieces so that the saw cut is precisely in the center of the hole. From 2-inch stock cut two pieces, one 8½x2¾ inches and one 8½x1¾ inches, and assemble as shown.

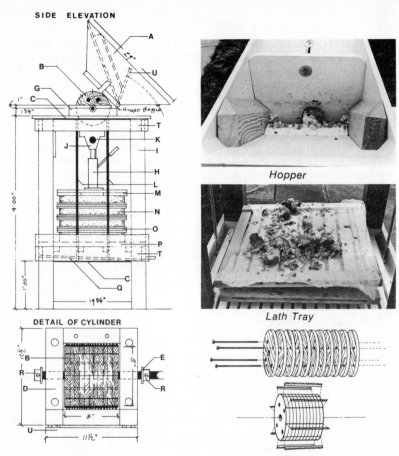

SIDE ELEVATION

DETAIL OF CYLINDER

Hopper

Lath Tray

Grater Cylinder

Grater—Part B

The grater cylinder consists of ¾-inch discs glued and bolted together to make an 8x8 cylinder. Bolt the assembly together with four bolts countersunk at each end, then file the cylinder until perfectly smooth. Drill a 1-inch hole through the center.

Mark the circumference of the cylinder into eighths and inscribe lines lengthwise on its surface. On each line make a saw cut into which the blades will be fitted (the depth of these cuts depends on the size of blades being used). In seven cuts, pieces of a coarse saw blade (such as a bucksaw or pruning saw) are placed with ³⁄₁₆ inch of teeth protruding from the cylinder. In the remaining cut, the blade is placed down so that a smooth edge protrudes to the same extent as the teeth.

Shaft—Part E

The shaft consists of a 23-inch piece of ¾-inch pipe. One-quarter inch holes are drilled at each end of the cylinder so that pins may be inserted to keep the cylinder from turning on the shaft. Attach collars

(R: ¾-inch lengths of 1-inch pipe with a set screw through one side) to the shaft to keep the cylinder properly spaced between the bearings. Mark bearing caps (D) so that they are in the same position as they were originally made.

Hopper—Part A

The hopper fits over the grater. Cut out notches on the bottom to fit over the bearing caps. The hopper may be removed for cleaning by releasing the 4-inch hook and eye at each end. The baffle board (U) is hinged at the bottom and can be adjusted to different positions by loosening the thumbscrew. The lower edge of the baffle board is tapered to a ¼-inch thickness, with the taper extending back 2¾ inches on the side of the baffle board facing the grater.

To make apples flow freely into the grater, two 16-inch pieces of 2x4, with 45-degree bevels cut on the top edge and approximate angles cut on the ends so that they fit against the baffle board, are fastened to the inner sides of the hopper.

Top Covering

The top of the press is covered with ¾-inch plywood, joined to the 2x4's with 3-inch screws in each corner.

Pressure Bar—Part K

A 1½-inch steel shaft is strong enough to handle most of the pressures used. However, if the pressure is great enough that the shaft is in danger of being bent, place a piece of 4x4 beneath the shaft. To keep the 4x4 from turning, notch out the top so that it fits around the support for the shaft (J).

Operating the Press

When you're ready to put the squeeze on your first batch of apples, place a piece of unbleached cheesecloth on the slatted rack (P) with the corners of the cloth in the middle of the sides of the rack. Drop apples into the hopper three or four at a time, and grate until the pulp forms a layer 2 to 3 inches thick and 18 inches square. Then fold the corners of the cloth over the pulp, completely enclosing the mass (commonly called a "cheese"). Place a lath tray (O) on top of this first layer and repeat the operation. With a short jack, you can press five cheeses at a time, yielding about ten gallons of juice. Place the pressure platform (M) on top of the last cheese and work the jack between this and the shaft (K).

To provide solid support for the top of the jack, have a 1-inch piece of 1¾-inch pipe welded to a 2-inch circle of ¼-inch flatiron. Then have this piece welded to the center of the bottom of the 1½-inch iron shaft.

A Durable
Orchard Ladder

A sturdy ladder is an invaluable orchard and woodlot tool, but it is also a fairly expensive tool. This truss ladder will not only shave that expense, it will be a challenging woodworking project for any homestead handyman. And its use doesn't need to be restricted to the orchard or woodlot.

This ladder was constructed, following an old design, using 1x2 material. The rungs should be hardwood; the uprights can be either hardwood or softwood. The ladder described here is 10 feet tall, but the design is adaptable for any length, 8 to 14 feet.

Just be sure to keep the bolts tight.

1. Rough-cut the rungs from 1x2 hardwood. You will need two 18 inches long, two 20 inches long, two 24 inches, one 27 and two 30 inches long. If you are using 12-foot lengths of hardwood, cut two feet off each of four boards, making four rungs and the uprights. A fifth 12-footer will yield the remainder of the necessary rungs.

2. Layout is half the battle in this project. Since the uprights are converging, the dadoes for the rungs must be cut on a slight angle. To determine the angle, lay out two of the uprights on your shop floor, with the bottom ends 30 inches apart, the tops 12 inches apart.

    To ensure that all is level and plumb, you should lay out the uprights in relation to a center line, whether it be an imaginary one or an actual chalk line drawn on the shop floor, and a bottom line—one perpendicular to the center line. Measure up to 12 inches along the center line and lay the first rung (a piece of 1x2) across the two uprights, making sure—through the use of a framing square—that it is perpendicular to the center line. Mark the uprights above and below the rung for the dado. Measure 12 inches up along the center line from the top of that first rung to the bottom of the second rung. Lay it in place and mark the uprights for dadoing. Keep repeating the process until the uprights are marked for all nine rungs.

3. Since you need four uprights altogether, mark a second pair, using the first pair as patterns. Remember that the uprights are mirror images—don't lay out one and use it as a pattern for the other three.

4. Cut all the dadoes ⅜-inch deep and 2 inches wide for rungs.

5. Lay out the uprights again, this time across sawhorses. Put the rungs in place and lay the second pair of uprights atop them. Now drill a ¼-inch hole through each joint of rung and uprights. Fasten the joints with 2½x¼-inch machine bolts, each with two washers.

6. After the ladder is completely assembled, trim off the excess rung material.

Materials

     5 pcs. 1x2-inch x 12-foot hardwood
     18-2½x¼-inch machine bolts with nuts and two
       washers each.

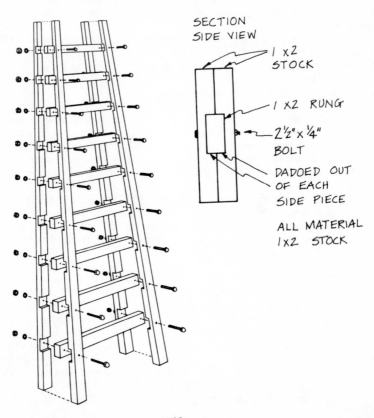

SECTION
SIDE VIEW

1 x2 STOCK

1 X2 RUNG

2½" x ¼" BOLT

DADOED OUT OF EACH SIDE PIECE

ALL MATERIAL 1x2 STOCK

Quick-Snip
Fruit Picker

When your fruit trees are ready for picking this fall, don't get a stiff neck staring up at the crop. And don't settle for bruised or overripened fruit because you waited until it hit the ground. Try this old-time remedy—make your own fruit picker. Once you get the knack of operating this homemade gadget, you may outstrip a champion handpicker.

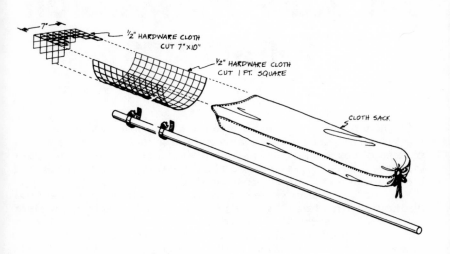

7"

½" HARDWARE CLOTH
CUT 7"x10"

½" HARDWARE CLOTH
CUT 1 FT. SQUARE

CLOTH SACK.

1. Cut a 1-foot-square piece of ½-inch hardware cloth, and 7x10-inch piece of ½-inch hardware cloth.
2. Cut the smaller piece into an "arrow" shape, with a notch on one 7-inch end and a tapered point on the other.
3. Form the square piece into a U-shaped trough. Using thin wire, fasten the smaller piece to the top of the trough, folding the "point" to enclose one end.
4. Using 1-inch hose clamps, fasten the resulting hardware-cloth basket to an 8- to 10-foot pole.
5. Cut the muslin in half, forming a sleeve of each piece, then sew the two together to form one long sleeve. Hem one end and attach to the hardware-cloth basket. Sew a large hem in the bottom, with drawstrings. This will permit you to collect in the sleeve.

Materials

1 piece ½-inch dowel, 8 to 10 feet
1 piece ½-inch hardware cloth, 21x36 inches
Wire
2-1-inch hose clamps
2 yards muslin

An "Add-On" Mansion for Martins

The benefits of attracting birds to your backyard are twofold. First, purple martins and many other species eat several times their weight in mosquitoes, codling moths and other garden pests. Second, your family will have the pleasant and educational experience of observing bird families go through their seasonal cycle.

You can provide for some backyard martins by making a special birdhouse with stories that come in attachable sections. A one-floor house will have eight ventilated rooms, but more uniform sections can be added to house an expanding colony. The roof, built to the same lateral dimensions, attaches to the top story. All sections are held together with hooks and screw eyes. To clean, just take the house apart and dump out the debris.

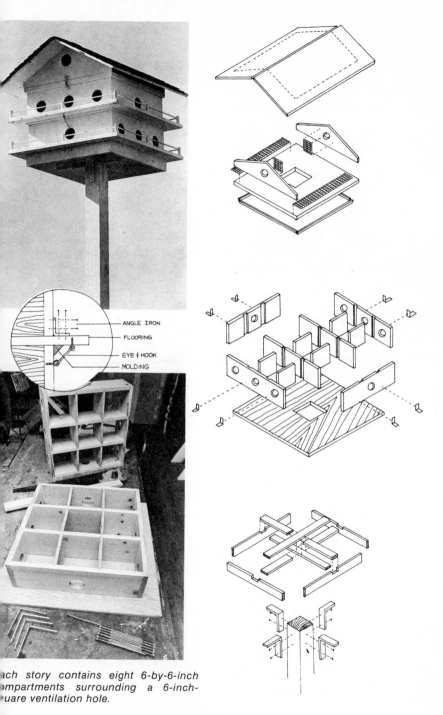

ANGLE IRON

FLOORING

EYE & HOOK

MOLDING

ach story contains eight 6-by-6-inch
ompartments surrounding a 6-inch-
uare ventilation hole.

43

One advantage this house has is ventilation. A central shaft and vents under the eaves and in the gable wall permit air to circulate.

The house should be situated in an open space. Like other swallows, purple martins are attracted by water, so there's a better chance you'll attract a colony if there is a pond or stream nearby.

The suggested construction plan is for a two-story house. Follow the same dimensions for adding other floors.

1. Cut pieces for roof as follows: two 16x29½-inch pieces of ½-inch exterior plywood, a 22¼-inch square floor, and two 6x20½-inch gable walls from ¾-inch exterior plywood (tapered to make a pitched roof from the peak to a point 1 inch up from each end).

2. Cut a 2-inch diameter hole in the center of each gable wall and cover it with window screen. Cut a 6-inch-square air-shaft hole in the center of the roof floor. Glue and nail (4d nails) the gable walls to the floor. Place screening along the 1-inch-high vent under eaves, stapling it first to the floor, then to the roof panels as they are attached. Assemble roof with glue and nails. Cut lightweight roofing paper and fasten to roof.

3. For one story, cut pieces of ¾-inch exterior plywood as follows: one 26½-inch-square floor, two 6x20½-inch walls, two 6x19-inch walls, two 6x19½-inch interior partitions. Cut six 6x6½-inch interior partitions from ½-inch exterior plywood.

4. Cut 2½-inch entrance holes and dadoes for the partitions. In the 20½-inch-long outside walls, cut three entrance holes, the first in the center of the wall, and another 6 inches to each side of the first. Cut a single hole in each of the 19-inch outside walls. Measure 7 inches from each end of the 20½-inch walls and mark the center line for ¾-inch-wide by ½-inch-deep dadoes. Measure 6¼ inches from each end of the 19-inch walls and mark the center line for a ½-inch-wide by ¼-inch-deep dado. Measure 6½ inches from each end of the 9½-inch-wide by ¼-inch-deep dadoes; mark both sides of the partition (dadoes must be cut in both sides) and cut all the dadoes. Lay out and cut a 6-inch-square air-shaft hole in the center of the floor panel.

5. Assemble the walls with glue, using nails where possible. Center the wall assembly on the floor panel, leaving a 3-inch porch around the outside of the walls, and attach it with two small angle irons on each wall. (These two steps must be duplicated for each additional story added to the house.)

6. A cove molding around the underside of the roof and each story holds the parts in alignment. Set up the house and cut molding to size. Then nail it below each porch and below the roof.

7. Connect the sections with one hook and eye on each of two sides on each section.

8. Construct the foundation as follows: build central cross with double thickness of 1x3 oak. Cut four pieces 19 inches long, and dado each in the center for a half-lap joint. Assemble two

44

crosses, then glue them together. The frame should be 1x3 pine, 20½ inches square, assembled from two 20½-inch and two 19-inch lengths, as shown. Attach four heavy angle irons to the crosspieces for fastening to the supporting pole.

9. A guardrail around each porch will prevent young martins from falling and provide a secure perch for all the birds. Construct a rail with ½- and ¼-inch dowel.

10. Mount the house atop a 16-foot 4x4 cedar post, cemented into a 4-foot-deep hole. Weighing more than 50 pounds, a two-story house is too heavy to mount on a hinged post. Instead, use a ladder for the annual cleanout, carrying the roof to the ground, then the top story, and finally the lower story.

Materials

Wood

    1–4x4-foot sheet ½-inch exterior plywood
    1 sheet ¾-inch exterior plywood
    1 piece cove molding 10 feet long
    1 piece cove molding 12 feet long
    1 piece 1x3x8-foot oak
    1 piece 1x3x8-foot pine
    1 piece 36x½-inch dowel
    8 pieces 36x¼-inch dowel
    1 piece 4x4x16-foot cedar (post)

Hardware

    1 piece 12x36-inch window screen
    Staples
    Glue
    4d nails
    Roofing paper (36 feet x 36 inches)
    16–2-inch angle irons w/screws
    6 hooks and eyes
    4–4-inch angle irons w/screws

A "Growlight" Planter Box

If you like to grow houseplants for their beauty, it's self-defeating to surround them with less-than-beautiful "gizmos" intended to make the plants grow and be beautiful. (Gizmos like fluorescent lights.) But you can conceal the light fixtures in a carefully constructed growlight stand that will blend right in with your best furniture. Basically, the light fixture is concealed inside a finished wooden box, which is suspended over a matching box—into which you place your plants—by wooden supports.

Of course, you can use part of this design and not all of it. You can construct "light boxes" to hang above your plants, wherever you locate them in your apartment or house. But this growlight plant stand was designed to be a self-contained plant display unit, and it looks best that way.

Construction

1. Cut the plywood into two pieces, each measuring 24 inches by 10⅝ inches. Cut the 1x8 and the 1x4 each into two 24-inch lengths and two 12-inch lengths.
2. Construct the plant box from the 1x8's and one piece of plywood. The 12-inch ends should overlap the 24-inch sides in a simple butt joint. The bottom should be flush. Glue and nail using 8d finishing nails. Predrilling holes in the ends will prevent splitting. The best sequence is to nail the sides to the bottom, then the ends to the sides and bottom. Countersink the nails and fill with wood putty.
3. Make and attach the feet to the plant box. Cut the 1x2 into four 6-inch pieces and four 3-inch pieces. Scallop each piece as shown at one end, and bevel the other at a 45-degree angle. Attach the feet to the bottom of the box as shown, the long

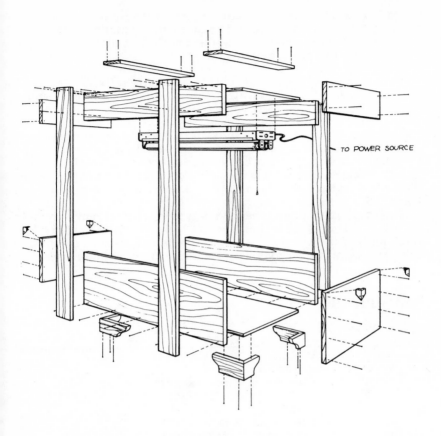

TO POWER SOURCE

pieces along the sides, the short along the ends. Glue and nail, driving 8d finishing nails through the feet and into the box.

4. Construct the light box in the same manner as the plant box, using the 1x4 and the remaining piece of plywood.

5. Cut four 29-inch lengths from the 1x3. Glue and nail these support struts to the light box, as shown two to a side, 3¾ inches from either end, driving 3d finishing nails through the side into the strut.

6. Measure for the remaining pieces of 1x3, which run across the top of the light box. They should be just about 13½ inches long. Glue and nail them in place.

7. Install the light fixture in the center of the light box.

8. Attach the light box to the plant box. The ends of the support struts should be flush with the bottom of the box, in line with the joint between the box and the feet.

9. Stain and/or varnish the stand. Apply a heavy coat (several coats would be best) of polyester resin to the inside of the plant box.

10. Attach the decorative corner pieces to the plant box (and to the light box, if you want). The corners are cut out of sheet metal and bent as shown. Paint them with flat paint, and when the paint has dried, nail them in place.

If you happen to have a longer fluorescent light fixture on hand, it should not be difficult to alter the dimensions of the stand to accommodate the fixture. If you have materials of slightly different dimensions, alter the stand as necessary to make use of them.

Of course, you can also alter the stand to accommodate more plants. You might want to use a two-tubed four-foot fixture. Thus, you'd want to make the sides of the plant box and the light box four feet long, rather than two feet long. And to completely conceal the fixture, you may have to use 1x6's, rather than 1x4's for the sides and ends on the light box.

Moreover, since plants respond best to the fluorescent light when they are but four to six inches from the light, you may want to reduce the length of the supporting struts. The length used in this design, however, seems to be a good compromise between providing adequate light and growing room.

Materials

Wood

1-2' by 4' sht.	¾" int. plywood or
Bottom and top:	2 pcs. 24" by 10⅝"
1 pc. 1x8x8' or	
Plant box sides:	2 pcs. 1x8x24"
ends:	2 pcs. 1x8x12"
1 pc. 1x4x8' or	
Light box sides:	2 pcs. 1x4x24"
ends:	2 pcs. 1x4x12"
1 pc. 1x2x4' or	
Feet:	4 pcs. 1x2x6"
	4 pcs. 1x2x3"
1 pc. 1x3x12' or	
Struts:	4 pcs. 1x3x29"
	2 pcs. 1x3x13½"

Hardware
Glue
8d finishing nails
Wood putty
3d finishing nails
1-24" double-tube fluorescent light fixture
Polyester resin
1 pc. sheet metal 4" by 4" or 4 pcs. 2" by 1⅞"
Flat-black paint
Decorative brass nails

Fluorescent Growing Stand

It isn't absolutely necessary to provide for adjustable light fixtures. It is just as reasonable to set up a fixture arrangement for the lights and plants.

Many growlight users, for example, set up shelves with a fixture above each one (usually fastened to the bottom of the shelf above). More than one plant lover has a growlight room in the house, with plant benches and fluorescent fixtures above them.

A fairly simple arrangement was devised for a limited number of plants by Richard F. Krause. Krause uses his to start vegetables indoors, but it serves equally well for housebound plants.

Construction

1. Cut each 1x8 into one 54-inch length and one 30-inch length.
2. Make a 15-inch-wide base by joining the two 54-inch-long boards with glue.
3. Use the 30-inch lengths to make T-shaped sides, as illustrated. Use your light fixture to guide you in shaping the tops of the supports. The supports do not need to be shaped as shown. Unmodified boards will serve as well to support the light. Drill a ¾-inch hole in one T for the light cord.
4. Cut four struts from the 1x3. Each is 17 inches long, tapered from a point at the top to 2½ inches at the base. Attach to the sides with glue and eight 1¼-inch #10 screws.
5. Attach sides and struts to base exactly the length of the light fixture, probably 48 inches. Use 1½-inch #10 screws.
6. Finish sides and base with oil stain, paint, or varnish. Install light fixture.

Materials

Wood

> 2 pcs. 1x8x8' or
>> *Base:* 2 pcs. 1x8x54"
>> *Sides:* 2 pcs. 1x8x30"
>
> 1 pc. 1x3x6' or
>> *Struts:* 4 pcs. 1x3x17"

Hardware

> 8-1¼" #10 screws
> 8-1½" #10 screws
> 1-48" double-tube fluorescent light fixture

Krause used one-inch pine throughout, but almost any lumber is suitable. The extent to which you wish your indoor garden to grow will determine the size of your stand. Remember, though, to allow a distance of about 25 inches from the base to fluorescent tubes so that there will be enough light for most plants.

Almost any lumber is suitable for construction, but remember to allow about 25 inches from the base to the fluorescent tubes.

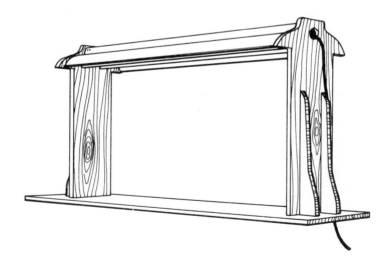

Mushroom Shelves for the Home Grower

Mushrooms are so good. When the mushroom shelves described here were completed, Rudy Keller, a gardener at the Organic Gardening Experimental Farm, volunteered to order some mushroom spawn and put them to the test. But he warned that few mushrooms would slip past his fast hand. "I love mushrooms."

And so do many other folks, people who have been buying mushrooms—when they could just as simply have been growing them. All that's needed is a dark, moist, cool place to locate trays or flats. A basement, a cold cellar or root cellar would be ideal spots. A flat or two would suffice.

But for families with an insatiable appetite for mushrooms, and for people who grow mushrooms for a supplemental income, something more elaborate is in order. Something like these mushroom shelves. You can build them in a short time. The space-saving, tier-shelf beds are easy to fill, empty, clean and disinfect.

Construct the uprights and crossbearers of rot-resisting cedar, redwood, cypress or pine.

The bed boards can be almost any dimensions that are convenient for you to work with and that will fit the space you have for your mushroom shelves. In our model, the beds measure 36 inches by 18 inches and are just over five inches deep.

Place the bottom bed six to eight inches away from the floor. Leave 18 inches between bed boards, and allow for from 24 inches to 30 inches between the top shelf bed and ceiling. The air will circulate easily. Place away from drafts and sunlight.

Fill the beds with five inches of good-quality horse manure and wheat straw compost. The final fermentation (peak heat) will destroy insect and fungus enemies. You may encourage it with artificial heat.

When the beds cool below 80 degrees and the pH is between 8.2 and 7.7, you are ready to plant the spawn. Purchase dry spawn of the prolific and disease-resistant brown variety from a commercial grower. Plant

When the mushrooms are ripe, harvest by grasping the stem and twisting.

spawn the size of a walnut every eight to ten inches, forming a diamond pattern one inch below the surface. Fill in the holes with compost.

From seven to 14 days after spawning, check to be sure a blue-gray color is "running" through the compost. Spread one inch of sterilized loam over the compost.

Keep the humidity between 70 and 80 percent and provide fans for good ventilation if possible.

Pinheads will appear from ten to 20 days after casing. Spray the beds lightly with water, maintain the humidity at 95 percent, and regulate the temperature between 60 and 65 degrees F.

Within six to eight weeks, mushroom clusters will appear. When the veils are stretched and they are ripe, harvest by grasping the stem and twisting. Cut out mushroom butts and fill the holes with ten parts of rich composted soil to one part lime. Beds maintained in this manner will last from two to five months before the medium is worn-out. To protect the following crop from fungus disease, the entire unit—shelves, walls, floors and tools—should be sterilized by steaming or scalding.

Construction

1. Cut legs and framing members from 2x2, four legs 47½ inches long, six end-pieces 15 inches long, and six side-pieces 34½ inches long.
2. Lay out the legs for dadoes to accept the side, (34½ inches long) framing members. The dadoes should be 1½ inches wide and ¾-inch deep. They should be 8¼ inches, 25¼ inches and 42¼ inches from the foot of the legs.
3. Assemble the frame. Lay out two of the legs with three of the side pieces and nail them together. Repeat with the remaining side pieces. Then nail the end-pieces in place. Use 8d nails.
4. Cut out the shelf bottom from ¾-inch exterior plywood. Each should measure 18 inches by 36 inches, with 1½-by-1½-inch notches at each corner. Nail the bottom in place, using 6d nails.
5. Rip the 1x8's to an actual width of 6 inches for the sides. You will need to rip 28 feet of material. Then cut six 36-inch long pieces and six 19½-inch long pieces. Nail the sides into place, using 6d nails. Nail through the sides into the bottoms, as well as into the support members, legs, and butting sides.

Materials

Wood

2 pcs. 2x2x8'	or	*Legs:* 4 pcs. 2x2x47½"
3 pcs. 2x2x10'	or	*End supports: 6 pcs.* 2x2x15"
		Side supports: 6 pcs. 2x2x34½"

2 pcs. 1x8x14'   or   *Sides:* 6 pcs. ¾" by 6" by 36"
                                        (act. meas.)
                            Ends: 6 pcs. ¾" by 6" by 19½"
                                        (act. meas.)
1 sht. ¾" ext. plywood or
                            Shelf bottoms: 3 pcs. 18" x 36"

Hardware
   8d nails
   6d nails

NOTE: If you want to make mushroom shelves similar to these, but lack the power equipment that makes ripping 28 feet of material a reasonable undertaking and that makes dadoes with a few passes, try this. Cut the legs 51¼ inches long. Skip the dadoes, merely mark the legs to position the framing members at 8¼ inches, 26½ inches, and 44¾ inches from the foot. Cut the side members 33 inches long and attach them to the legs with a simple butt joint. When it comes time to cut and attach the sides, use the full-size 1x8 lumber.

An even more simple design would be to construct the beds and attach the four legs to them.

If you want to enlarge the beds, remember to keep them less than an arm's length wide, unless you will locate them in a spot that allows access from either side. And remember as the bed-size increases, the weight of the compost-filled beds will be increasing. You may find it wise to use 2x3's or 2x4's and larger nails for framing.

A Fan Trellis for Climbing Ornamentals

When it comes to designing a trellis for clematis, climbing roses and other ornamentals, you'll want to give as much consideration to appearance as to utility. Here's a pair of small, traditional-type trellises that will do wonders for that blank garage or tool shed wall.

Construction

1. With a 31-inch piece of ¾-inch by 2½-inch knot-free white pine, mark and drill holes for the dowel rods and carriage bolt, as illustrated.
2. Using a power saw, rip the board into strips of equal thickness (approximately ³⁄₁₆ inch, depending on the width of your saw cut).
3. Fasten the carriage bolt in the lower hole and insert the three ¼-inch dowel rods. Nail the center strip to the dowels, then spread the outside strips to a distance of approximately 11 inches from center. Nail these outside strips to the dowels. Spread the remaining strips uniformly and fasten securely to the dowels.
4. For the stake, cut a nine-inch piece of ¾-inch stock and sharpen one end. Fasten this to the lower part of the trellis with two 1½-inch #10 wood screws.

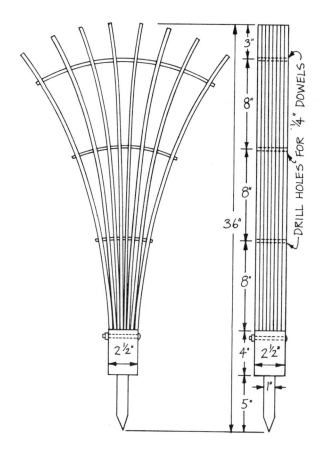

A Small Garden Trellis

This entire trellis can be made from 12½ feet of ½- by 1-inch white pine.

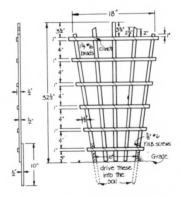

Construction

1. For the upright members, cut five pieces 32½ inches long.
2. The six horizontal pieces are 14, 15½, 16½, 18, 19½, and 20½ inches. Be careful to make both sides symmetrical, and see that the spacing of the horizontal pieces is equal.
3. Assemble the pieces with galvanized shingle-nails. It's easier to cut the pieces to exact size after the trellis is put together.
4. For the stakes, fasten two sharpened 10-inch pieces to the bottom of the trellis with screws and drive into the ground.

This type trellis usually requires some support at the upper end. A good method is to drill holes for screws in the wall and attach the trellis with a piece of ½-inch rod or strap-iron bent into a bracket.

A Trellis for Trailing Berry Vines

They are most valuable when built to last.

I have raised trailing-type berries (dew, boysen, logan, young and CASCADE) at the several different locations where we have lived. My original efforts at trellis-making left much to be desired, but each time I made a new one I added ideas till eventually the most important features of berry culture were provided for.

My notion of a good berry trellis has the following characteristics:

1. Hold the vines off the ground to allow easy access to the soil and to provide for easy picking of the berries.
2. Spread and distribute the foliage to provide shade for the berries, thereby preventing sunburn and false ripening prior to full maturation.
3. Space the vines for easy pruning and berry picking. I have never been content with the old-fashioned method of stringing the vines on single wires.
4. Make it easy to separate the bearing vines from the new ones without entanglement and without leaving the new ones lying on the ground.
5. Facilitate the removal of the old, no-longer-useful vines.

In making a permanent trellis, I prefer not to use wooden posts if I can get my hands on some scrap pipe, angle iron or old steel posts. Of course, if metal is not readily available, creosoted lumber can be used, with occasional replacement anticipated.

Through trial and error, I've learned that the best height for the upper deck of the trellis illustrated here is about 4½ feet. Position the second deck two feet below the upper one.

Be liberal with the portion of the post buried in the ground. I make mine 16 inches deep. If you fix a wooden post with concrete, do not encase the bottom end in the concrete. Leave an inch exposed to the earth and rot will not occur as rapidly.

The longitudinal member (I call it a stiffener) should be attached firmly to all the posts in the row, especially to the end posts.

Let the width of the decks be determined by how far you can reach without having to stretch uncomfortably. You will be working from both sides and should reach a little more than halfway across, so the total width should probably not exceed 30 inches.

The line wires of the fencing should be spaced four to six inches apart. Six- or 12-inch spacing is suitable for the stay wires. Avoid woven chicken wire—it's not strong enough and openings are too small for easy removal of old vines.

If your fencing is made of strands less than 12 gauge, add a single strand of heavier wire placed at the ends of the cross-arms for reinforcement.

If the supporting members are made of metal, bolts can be used if necessary, but it's far better to have them welded on. Plastic pipe clamps serve well for attaching the stiffener to the supports, which should be spaced about eight feet apart.

When your trellis is complete and the time is at hand to plant your vines, remember that another opportunity for deep tillage and fertilization will not arise without replanting the bed, so make an extra effort to do a good job the first time. As the bed is prepared

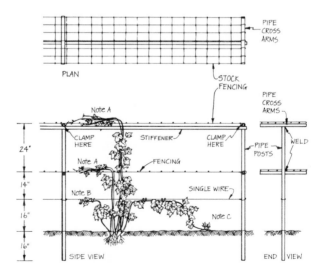

Optimum height for a trellis of this type is about 4½ feet. Determine width by how far you can reach into the vines without having to stretch uncomfortably—roughly 24 to 30 inches. By spreading and distributing the foliage to provide shade for berries, this trellis configuration wards off sunburn and false ripening.

directly under the center of the trellis, leave a slight depression for watering. Let the size of this trough be determined roughly by how much irrigation you will have to do in your locality.

I like to place my plants no more than 30 inches apart in the rows. Many nurserymen will frown upon this spacing as being too close, but since I fertilize and mulch heavily with manure compost, and since I never keep more than four canes from any one plant, I like to get as many healthy root systems started in the row as possible. This method gives me more berries by having more plants, but I do have to provide for added food. The force-feeding produces berries that are invariably bigger, sweeter and juicier than normal. Rows six feet apart are quite practical.

When my newly planted vines reach a length of about two feet, I tie them temporarily to the low single strand of wire to keep them up off the ground. Then, when the vines have grown a bit longer, I pick out the thriftiest ones for training up through the wire decks. They are directed out on the supporting fencing and as they continue to grow they are woven into the wire meshes. Less vigorous vines are removed so as to enhance the growth of the ones to be trained up.

As further growth takes place, I clip off the vine tips to promote branching. Later, the branched tips can be clipped again so rebranching will take place and cause the trellis decks to be completely covered. If things have gone well, your vines should be snuggly entwined with the fencing by the time the winter dormant season arrives. If your climate dictates, a suitable cover can be provided to protect against freezes.

The same process takes place each spring. Vines are restricted to the single wire till the berries are picked and the old vines are removed, then the training process is repeated. When it comes time to remove the old vines after they have produced their crop, I cut them off just below the bottom deck of the trellis and wait for their leaves to dry. This makes it considerably easier to remove the old canes, especially if you go through the blanket of drying vines and cut them into short sections.

If you have to put in a fill-in plant or if you wish to buy the least number of plants at first and expand later, leave one of the excess new vines on the single wire until it is long enough to touch the ground in the desired spot for the new plant. Then pin down the vine or weight it. Set it in a depression as if it were a transplant. I wait to cut the new plant loose until the vine feeding it has gone through its fruiting stage and needs to be removed. This is the routine that is encountered in nature, and since the best berries come from the best and largest root systems, I let the new plant be forced-fed from the parent vine as well as its own roots.

For temporary fastening of vines to the supporting wires I use a clip made from a six-inch piece of #14 gauge electric solid-strand wire with the insulation jacket left on. First bend the piece at its center so the two ends are parallel and about ¾ inch apart. Then bend the two ends back over themselves in a like manner. To use, just place the clip over the vine so it is cradled in the center bend and clip both hooks over the wire. When the ends are pressed down, they will hold in place until they are no longer necessary, at which point they can easily be removed and kept for reuse.

I feed my berry vines twice a year—once just after training the new vines up so as to promote their growth, and again at the end of the fall growing season, when a heavy compost mulch is provided to protect and feed the roots all winter. You'll know that you are doing a good job if an inspection in the spring shows the roots are plump and meaty. Thin, stringy roots indicate inadequate soil enrichment.

Water enough to enhance the leaching of nutrients and minerals out of the topsoil into the root zone for plant use. I also water extra during the ripening time to produce the juiciest berries possible. Some years this approach has produced berries twice the size of my neighbors. When picking fully ripe berries for home use, I found I couldn't use a bucket any larger than a gallon without having them crush themselves due to their own weight.

Fred W. Pontig

A Greenhouse You Will Dig

Plant at ground level, rather than above it, and your greenhouse heating problems are half solved.

I like to stay in my garden so much that I seldom get out to earn money. So when it came time to somehow put up a greenhouse for early-spring starter plants, I felt like the poor guy in the comics with his pockets turned inside out. I was broke, but not broken!

Somewhere in the foggy past I remembered reading of a trench-type greenhouse, where the walkway between the benches was a trench about three feet deep. The original ground level on either side of the trench served as benches. Basically, all one would be doing would be building a rather large hotbed with a trench to walk in.

I have a shovel and maddox, so it cost me nothing but an afternoon of hard work to get the trench dug. I made the house only ten feet long, with the trench eight feet long. The extra two feet made up a bench at the end of the walkway.

I built a very simple vertical wall by sinking two used railroad ties ($4 each here in Arkansas) about 30 inches into the ground and walling it up with old tongue-and-groove decking that Nancy had rescued from a house being torn down. This siding was free for the taking.

60

Simplicity and economy were the prerequisites for the author's curved-wall design. Curved struts and the 2-by-4 framing were covered with six-mil polyethylene.

Next we staked down a rough but adequate framework of cedar 2x4's on the ground. While Nancy was doing this, I went back into the trench and sided it up with some sawmill log slabs (free around here) and six metal fence posts. I drove the 5½-foot posts 2½ feet into the ground, three on each side, just far enough from the trench wall to slide in the log slabs and fasten them into position with flexible wire.

By now Nancy had improvised a simple framework and was carefully bending the ten-foot, 1x2 pine struts into place, hooking one end into notches on the top of the north wall and snapping the other end behind the front frame 2x4 that was staked three feet south of the trench's edge. The wall in the back (north) was put two feet behind the trench, so the front "bench" was three feet wide and the rear two feet wide.

To keep the struts from getting "wobbly knees," I joined them together with another 1x2 running the length of the greenhouse, about midway down the struts. I used wire to secure this brace to the curved struts. The ends of the 1x2 are nailed to the double 2x4 upright that serves as the door frame.

With the struts firmly in place, we finished framing by improvising end-pieces—a door into the trench on the west end and vents on each end.

Next, we covered the entire exterior with a sheet of six-mil clear plastic, then hauled in some crushed rock for the otherwise muddy trench. Soon we had the whole thing buttoned up well enough so that I could start setting in flats for the spring seedlings I needed.

Now about heating. Our weather here in the northwest Arkansas section of the Ozark Mountains is fickle at best and whacky at worst. In our four years here we've seen weeks of warm weather in February with flowers abloom, only to be followed by a March that was colder and nastier than any part of the winter prior.

By the time we finished the greenhouse, it was getting into one of these premature springs; so I didn't try to heat the house. I used it like a walk-in cold frame. When a cold snap finally hit us, and nighttime temperatures dropped back into the 20's, I ran an extension cord out our back door to the greenhouse and left two 250-watt brooder lamps burning overnight. I also draped two muslin sheets over the plastic. The inside temperature never dropped below 36 degrees.

Before a prospective greenhouse builder decides on the trench-type structure, consideration should be given to drainage at the site. Our backyard gets very soggy in wet weather. Still, the greenhouse was built on a slope steep enough so that I could dig a drainage channel and insert cheap concrete drain tiles. Now as ground moisture and irrigation water enter the house, it easily drains through the gravel floor and out the tiles. This would be rough to do on level land unless subsoil drainage is good.

I've found that the greenhouse keeps pretty warm on its own. Like a root cellar in winter, the soil is slow to give up its heat, and, with sunny days to reheat the soil, temperatures around freezing pose no problems.

I hope that a builder would give his or her best to finding and using salvage material. I have always loved this sport, and find that the longer I do it, the better I get. We managed to build this greenhouse for under $50.

And here's the best part. The greenhouse enabled me to set out early romaine and looseleaf lettuce crops that earned me nearly $100 at the local farmers' market.

"You didn't grow that here, did you?" was a common remark about lettuces that easily surpassed supermarket offerings in quality and earliness. Needless to say, my head as well as my wallet swelled, and the hours I spend in this little trench fortress are delightful.

Mike Milligan

Another Curved-Wall Greenhouse

Sooner or later, everyone who contemplates building an energy-conserving greenhouse is forced to confront the same question: Granted, all greenhouses lose their heat due to lack of insulation, but how do you insulate a transparent structure? Using two layers of plastic, glass or other clear material helps a great deal but loss through convection still takes place. The only real answer is to heavily insulate the north wall as well as the east and west walls.

The shape we decided on accommodates this approach quite well, leaving the southern curved section clear from the shelf back to the north wall. We then designed and built two sliding insulated (with sprayed-in-place polyurethane foam) panels that meet, in rolltop-desk fashion, when closed to totally insulate the clear area. The east and west walls are built with 2x4 construction and have plywood on both sides with plastic foam insulation between. The outside was painted and the insides were covered with reflective mylar to reflect as much light as possible onto the plants.

The north wall was also built from 2x4's, plywood and insulation, but it was made one foot thick and became the heat storage wall. It is filled with 4½ tons of river gravel. A blower located in the greenhouse circulates the warm air inside through the rocks and heats them all day when the sun is out. At night, after the insulated panels are closed, the blower may be turned on to bring the heat back into the greenhouse.

This worked well enough so that during the winter of 1976 (October—March) our electric bill for running the greenhouse (lights, heat cables for seedlings, the blower and an auxiliary electric heater set at 55 degrees F that come on when the solar system failed) was only $24.70! This surely makes winter vegetable production economical. I kept my cactus collection and a few other plants in the greenhouse and started around 3,000 vegetable transplants to sell.

The greenhouse can also be used year-round with no summer overheating. There are vents in the top of the north wall, and the blower

Two sliding, insulated panels meet in rolltop-desk fashion to completely insulate the clear area when closed. Gravel in the north wall stores warmth in winter, coolness in summer.

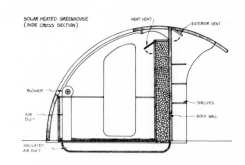

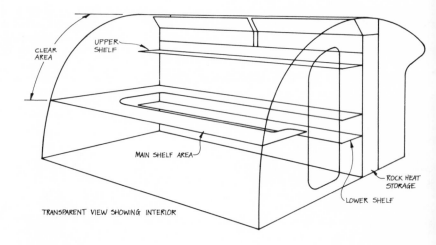

TRANSPARENT VIEW SHOWING INTERIOR

can be turned on to pull the warm air through the rocks cooling it. I also installed a shade cloth which keeps the temperature below 100 degrees even on very hot, sunny days.

Materials for the structure cost around $1,500 (in 1976), but corners could be cut. The polyurethane insulation is very expensive; another type could be used. Also the plexiglass glazed area could be a translucent fiberglass, although the clear is nice to look through. But you must consider the fuel savings and the cost of this greenhouse over many years as it is a permanent-type structure that should be in service for quite some time.

Ellen Jantzen

Build Your Own Lime Spreader

Here's a device to ease the chore of spreading lime and rock fertilizers on a large garden. The spreader is not difficult to make and the hopper can be expanded or shrunk to serve the user or the materials at hand.

The model constructed in the OGF Workshop features homemade wooden wheels, but the plan could accommodate manufactured wheels.

Construction

1. The wheels are fabricated from 1x12 stock. Cut eight 20-inch lengths, four being used for each wheel. Select a scrap strip of wood at least 10 inches long and drive two nails through it 9 inches apart. This will be used to scribe the wheel. Lay out two of the 1x12 boards, their long dimensions abutting. Locate the center of the wheel 10 inches from either end and 1½ inches from the joint between the two boards. The idea is to avoid the weakness that would result from having the wheels' center hubs falling in the joint of the two boards. Using the homemade scriber, mark off the diameter of the wheel. After cutting out this first wheel with a coping saw or jigsaw, use it as a pattern for scribing and cutting the remaining four units. Using 1½-inch #10 screws, glue and screw together two wheels, each comprised of two units. In doing so, align the joints perpendicular to each other for additional strength.

2. The hopper is made of 1x10 stock. Cut two 30½-inch lengths for the front and back, two 11⅛-inch lengths for the ends, and a 32-inch length for the bottom. Clamp the end-pieces together and along one edge measure 2½ inches from one corner and mark; then along the same edge measure 2⅝ inches from the other

corner and mark. Draw a line from the marks to the nearest corners on the other edge of the board, then cut along the lines. This procedure will give the ends the appropriate shape, as shown. Drill a 1-inch diameter hole 2 inches from the bottom center of the end boards. Rip the bottom to an actual 6-inch width.

3. The axle is made from a 36-inch length of 1-inch dowel. Measure and mark 3 inches from each end of the dowel, then drill eight ¼-inch holes through the dowel, evenly spacing them *between* the marks and alternating the plane of the holes. Cut eight 3-inch lengths of ¼-inch dowel and drive a piece through each hole in the axle, leaving an inch protruding on each end of the hole. Make a saw kerf 1½ inches deep in each end of the axle.

4. Cut two 9¼-inch lengths of 2x4 for the handle mounting. Measure 11⁷⁄₁₆ inches from each end of the hopper back and scribe a line across the board. Attach the two pieces of 2x4 to the back, one piece flush with each line. The 2x4's should be 7⅝ inches apart. Use glue and three 2-inch #10 screws in each 2x4, driving the screws through the back into the 2x4's.

5. Assemble the hopper using glue and 8d nails. The ends overlap the front and back. Be sure to slip the ends over the axle as you butt them against the front and back; you won't be able to install the axle after the hopper is fastened together. Also, be sure the bottom edges of the boards are flush, so you can seal the bottom without leaks. You will probably find it desirable, therefore, to bevel the bottom edge of the back and front to give them a broader flat surface on the bottom. Use a sliding T-bevel to duplicate the angle of the end-pieces on the butt end of the front and back board, then join the butt-end marks across the faces of the boards and place the edge to the line. Nail the bottom in place.

6. Make the handle assembly. Cut two 36-inch lengths and one 19-inch length of 2x3. Using a wood rasp or drawknife, round 4½ inches at each end of the 19-inch 2x3 to form comfortable hand-grips. Then cut two 1½-inch-wide and ½-inch-deep dadoes in each broad face of the 19-inch piece, locating them an equal distance—about 6⅝ inches—from each end of the 2x3, the outer edges 7⅝ inches apart. Fit the butt end of a 36-inch 2x3 into each dado and fasten with glue and two 1½-inch #10 screws. Cut the free ends of the handle assembly on such an angle that the grips will be at a comfortable height when the spreader is assembled. The angle must be fairly acute. Then slip the handle assembly between the mountings and drive two 1½-inch #10 screws through each mounting member into the handle shaft. Fasten in place with a total of four 1½-inch #10 screws.

7. The flow of lime is controlled by a sliding panel that covers or exposes holes drilled in the hopper bottom.

   a. Cut a 30¼-inch-long by 7-inch-wide piece of ¼-inch plywood. Cut two 6½-inch lengths of 1x1 stock and cut a

⁵⁄₁₆-inch-wide by ⁵⁄₁₆-inch-deep rabbet in each piece. Glue and nail these 1x1 guides to the bottom edges of the hopper end-pieces, with the rabbet on the upper inside edge of the guide.

Slide the plywood panel into the guides and fasten ¼-inch by ¾-inch strips 7 inches long to each end of the plywood, abutting the guide. These strips will hold the plywood panel in proper alignment, which makes it easier to slide back and forth, adjusting the lime flow. Attach a ¼-inch by ¾-inch strip 31¾ inches long to the lower front edge of the hopper, so it slightly overlaps the bottom edge and acts as a stop for the sliding panel.

b. Now cut a 31-inch and a 12-inch piece of 1x1 hardwood stock for the control lever. Cut a 1-inch tenon at one end of the 12-inch piece and a 1½-inch-deep notch in one end of the 31-inch piece; the width of the notch should be slightly greater than the thickness of the tenon. Slip the two together, forming a right angle, then drill a ¼-inch hole and fasten the two pieces together with a 1½-inch-long ¼-inch bolt (with washers). Drill a similar hole 15 inches from the other end of the 31-inch piece. Measure 15 inches from the hopper end of one handle shaft and drill a ½-inch hole in the handle. Fit a bolt through the handle and the lever, then position the short rod across the sliding panel. Mark the position and drive ¾-inch #6 screws through the plywood into the level rod. Use a 4-inch-long ¼-inch bolt

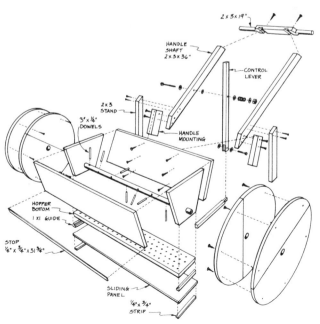

to attach the control lever, placing washers between the bolt head and handle, handle and lever, lever and a spring, and spring and nut.

Finally, drill ⅜-inch holes in the hopper bottom (but not in the sliding panel). Drill them in several alternating rows so that you can vary the flow from slow to fast by uncovering more holes.

8. Attach the wheels. Daub epoxy glue on the axle shaft and slip the wheels onto the axle. Drive a small wedge, cut from scrap, into the saw kerf in each end of the axle.

9. Hold the spreader in a standing position and measure from the handle shafts to the ground. Cut two lengths of 2x3 to this length and attach them to the handle shafts. They will be about 16½ inches long. Cut the corner that projects above the top of the handle shaft flush.

Materials

Wood

Wheels: 8 pcs. 1x12x20″
Hopper:
  Front and back: 2 pcs. 1x10x30½″
  Ends: 2 pcs. 1x10x11⅛″
  Bottom: 1 pc. 1x10x32″
Axle: 1 pc. 36″ x 1″ dowel
Pins: 8 pcs. 3″ x ¼″ dowel
Handle mount: 2 pcs. 2x4x9¼″
Handle: 2 pcs. 2x3x36″
  1 pc. 2x3x19″
  2 pcs. 2x3x16½″
Flow control board: 1 pc. 30¼″ x 7″
  (¼″ ext. plywood)
Flow control board tracks:
  (hardwood) 2 pcs. 1x1x6½″
Control lever: 1 pc. 1x1x31″
  1 pc. 1x1x12″
Stop: 2 pcs. ¼″x¾″x7″
  1 pc. ¼″x¾″x31¾″

Hardware

8d nails
White glue
24-1½″ #10 screws
3-2″ #10 screws
1-1½″ x ¼″ bolt w/nut and washers
4-¾″ #6 screws
1-4″ x ¼″ bolt w/nut and washers
1-2″ coil spring
Epoxy glue

This plan is excerpted from BUILD IT BETTER YOURSELF, published by Rodale Press, Inc., April, 1977.

An Outside Firewood Rack You Can Build

This rack is made entirely from rough-sawn green hardwood 2x4's and 2x6's.

The size of the rack can be adapted to suit your own needs by changing the length of the sides, but one larger than the illustrated model would probably be impractical. All the wood used here was run over a jointer on all sides and the edges rounded with a router, but the wood could also be used in its rough state if a more rustic appearance is desired.

Construction

1. To make the larger model you will need seven 2x4's by 8 feet and one 2x6 by 12 feet. Cut six pieces of 2x4 four feet long, with a 30-degree angle on each side. Cut four pieces of 2x4 four feet long, with a 30-degree angle on one end.
2. Cut angle lap joints on both ends of the six pieces and on one end of the four pieces. This requires the removal of half the depth of the stock to a width of two inches at the same 30-degree angle.
3. Join the two sets of five pieces together using two 2½-by-⅜-inch carriage bolts and washers at each joint, making sure to have the pieces without the angle lap joint on either end at the bottom.
4. Cut the 2x6 to the dimension shown.
5. To find the positions and angles for the dadoes on the bases and end-pieces, lay the two assembled pieces on a flat surface, one on top of the other, and adjust the pieces so that they are exactly the same. Position one base piece underneath the bottom and space evenly from ends, then scribe the lines on the base and frame at intersections. Use a bevel square to transfer

the angles to the other piece, then remove the wood between the lines to one-half the depth of the stock by making repeated cuts.

6. Attach the bases to the frame with two 2½-by-⅜-inch carriage bolts and washers at each joint.

7. Adjust the distance between the two assembled frames to meet your needs; the one shown here has a space of 16 inches. Cut seven 16-inch pieces from the remaining 2x4's, position midway between each joint and fasten with two 3½-by-⁵⁄₁₆-inch lag screws and washers. Finally, take two additional pieces of 2x4, space them evenly on the bases and fasten them in similar fashion.

8. Apply an oil stain to the rack to help preserve the wood.

Materials

Wood
> 10-2″x4″x4′ hardwood for frame
> 2-2″x6″x6′ hardwood for base
> 7-2″x4″x16″ hardwood for cross braces

Hardware
> 24-2½″x⅜″ carriage bolts
> 28-3½″x⁵⁄₁₆″ lag screws
> 52 washers for above

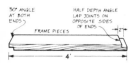

The wood of the finished rack can be rough or smooth, but an oil stain should be applied to help preserve it.

A TUBULAR STEEL WOOD RACK

Here's a tubular steel version that can store up to one-third cord of wood neatly and attractively. Its design employs two sizes of square steel tubing—a heavy (nine-gauge) tubing for legs and bottom rails, and a lighter tubing for bridging and side-bar assembly. Do-it-yourselfers with even very modest welding skills will probably want to tackle the welding themselves. Otherwise, the local blacksmith or welding shop should be able to put it together for you for under $20.

The lighter tubing for the bridging and side-bar assembly should have an outside diameter that will slip into the heavier legs, thereby permitting a lighter rack and reducing the strain on the leg-bottom welds. The side bars of the model shown are ten feet long, bottom rails are four feet, bridging and legs are 12 inches.

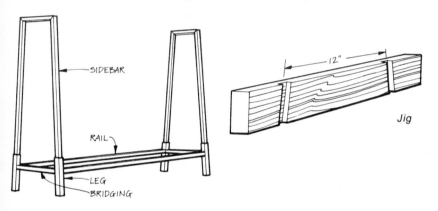

Jig

Construction

1. Wooden 2x4 jigs come in handy when you're ready to assemble for welding. Cut 1-inch-deep grooves 12 inches apart on 2½-degree angles, making the grooves just wide enough to provide a close fit for the larger tubing.
2. Use a 5-foot gluing clamp to hold the legs and bottom rails in place when you're ready to weld. Clamp the wooden jigs to the legs four inches from the top of each leg. This is the same point at which the top side of the bottom rail should be welded to the leg. Mark legs both front and back and weld.
3. Next, insert the 12-inch bridging pieces between the legs, one-half inch from the tops of the legs. Wooden jigs will help hold the legs and permit the bridging to be pulled up and wedged in place. Weld the bridging pieces.
4. Finally, slip the side bars into the legs, clamp the tops of the side-bar assembly in place with C clamps, tack weld, remove the clamps and finish weld. File or grind these top welds for smooth appearance and remove slag from the welds with hammer and wire brush.

Rustic Garden Furniture

Wouldn't it be splendid if somebody came up with some alternative to those short-lived, pastel vinyl wonders that pass for lawn and garden furniture these days? Well, they have, or rather you can, with nothing more than a hammer, saw and some rough-sawn boards and poles cut from saplings. Leave the redwood in California—these attractive, durable tables and chairs are meant to be made of native species direct from your own woodlot or local lumber supplier.

RUSTIC BENCH

This strong and serviceable garden bench is made using only saw, hammer and simple T-joint. The wood should be straight and approximately two to three inches thick. All nails used are 20d or 30d commons, and it would be a good idea to apply a wood preserver to all joints.

Construction

1. Cut four legs 12 inches long and saw shallow V-notches at the top of each. Each pair, front and rear are T-jointed to a crossrail one foot shorter than the overall length of the bench. Fasten these rails 3 inches above the ground.
2. To construct the seat take two lengths of rustic pole, V-notch both ends horizontally, and T-joint them to a short piece in the middle. The exact length of this spacer will depend on the thickness of the rustic pole, but the overall width of the seat should be 12 to 13 inches.
3. Nail end-pieces approximately 13 inches long across the ends of the seat; then nail the seat into the V-notches at tops of legs.
4. Between the bottom rails fit two suitably cut lengths of rustic pole well-nailed from front and back.

Exploded diagram shows construction details for the rustic bench.

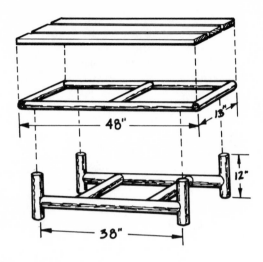

5. The seat planks are 3¾-by-1⅛-inch rough-sawn boards. Space equally and nail with 8d common nails. Sand lightly to remove snags and treat all exposed wood with linseed oil.

Materials

Quantity	Size and Description	Purpose
4	3" dia. x 12"	legs
2	3" dia. x 38"	crossrails
2	3" dia. x 15"	braces between bottom crossrails
2	2" dia. x 48"	seat frame
1	2" dia. x 8"	seat frame
2	2" dia. x 13"	seat frame
3	3¾ x 1 x 48"	seat

Note: Also several 30d, 20d and 8d common nails and linseed oil.

RUSTIC TABLE

Construction

1. Cut four legs 36 inches long from 3-inch-diameter logs. Saw their upper ends into shallow V-notches and their lower ends with a 45-degree slope. Join them at the middle with a crossover joint and nail from both sides with 30d nails.

2. Cut two pieces 48 inches long and attach at V-notches. Then cut a length of pole approximately 2 inches in diameter and 48 inches long and nail it to the undersides of the crossover leg joints.
3. For the tabletop, use rough-sawn lumber, cut into lengths approximately 2 inches longer than the distance between the poles nailed to the V-notches. Sand the top surface to remove splinters and round edges with wood rasp. Apply linseed oil as a preservative to tabletop and joints.

Materials

Quantity	Size and Description	Purpose
4	3" dia. x 36"	legs
2	2" dia. x 48"	tabletop nailers
1	2" dia. x 48"	bottom crossover
6 to 8	1" x 36" x random	top

Note: It is best to use a softwood such as pine or poplar. You'll also need several 30d and 20d nails and about ½ pound of 8d common nails.

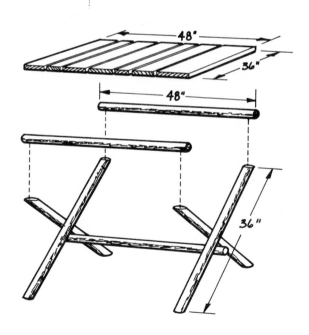

Sturdy X-frame base of table is topped by crossboards, three feet wide.

RUSTIC CHAIR

Construction

1. Cut four pieces of rustic pole 20 inches long and 3 inches in diameter for the legs. Next cut four pieces of 2-inch-diameter pole—two pieces 16½ inches for side crossrails, one piece 20½ inches, and one piece 16 inches.
2. Saw shallow V-notches in both ends of the four pieces.
3. Nail the side pieces in place 11 inches from the bottom using 30d common nails. Then position and nail the front and back braces, the front being 14 inches from the bottom and the back 16 inches.

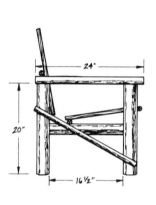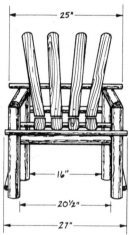

Overall rear width is 25 inches. Note 4½-inch difference in spacing between the front and back legs.

4. Make the two armrests by splitting a 24-inch piece of 3-inch-diameter stock in half lengthwise. (This piece should be free from large knots for easier splitting.) Nail these to the tops of the legs, leaving 1½-inch overhang in front.
5. Saw a length of approximately 1¼-inch pole into the following sections: two pieces 25½ inches for side braces, one piece 25 inches for top chair back support, one piece 26 inches for back seat support, and one piece 27 inches to be nailed flush with the seat boards.
6. Secure the 26-inch seat support to the side braces 7 inches from the back. Next, nail in place the 25½-inch pieces to the legs at an angle approximately 3 inches from the bottom in front and 12 inches from the bottom in back, making sure to fit snugly underneath previously nailed piece. Fasten the 25-inch piece on the top of the back of the armrests, directly over the legs (note: use 10d nails).

7. Cut the seat and backrest from 2¼-by-1-inch rough-sawn wood and sand well to remove splinters. Cut the four seat pieces 16 inches long and the four backrest pieces 19 inches. Round off the front edges of the seat and the tops of the backrest with a wood rasp. Nail the seat and backrest boards to their proper supports using 8d nails. Splay the tops of the backrest and the front of the seat boards slightly outward.

8. Finally, nail the 27-by-1¼-inch piece to the legs, being careful to position the top edge flush with the tops of the seat boards. If bark has been removed, apply linseed oil to the entire chair.

Materials

Quantity	Size and Description	Purpose
4	3″ dia. x 20″	legs
1	3″ dia. x 24″	armrests
2	2″ dia. x 16½″	side crossrails
1	2″ dia. x 20½″	front crossrail
1	2″ dia. x 16″	back crossrail
2	1¼″ dia. x 25½″	side angle braces
1	1¼″ dia. x 25″	chair back support
1	1¼″ dia. x 27″	front seat edge
1	1¼″ dia. x 26″	back seat support
4	2¼ x 1 x 16″	seat
4	2¼ x 1 x 19″	backrest

Make a Gathering Basket

What sort of container do you grab when you head for the garden or orchard to gather your harvest? For years we used cardboard boxes, paper sacks, or, in an emergency, a hat. The box allowed the fruit to roll around and bruise; the bag burst when too heavily loaded; and the hat was completely unsuitable. We felt that there had to be a better way.

During a visit to Williamsburg, Virginia, we saw beautifully handwoven baskets made of oak splits. As crafts go, oak split basketry

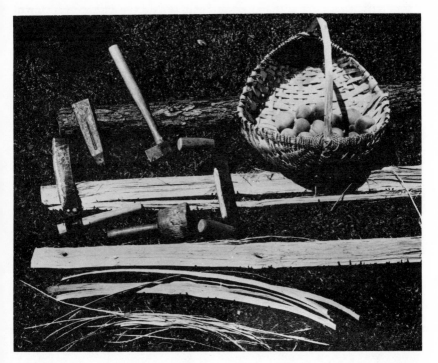

A large basket and the tools and materials needed to make it include thin splits, heavy short splits for ribs, two eighth sections of log, and a half log with the bark on. The tools include froe, mallet, drawknife, steel wedge and hammer.

is fairly simple; the results are pleasing, and the raw materials are available in most of the United States.

To get started, you need a white oak log about six inches in diameter and six to eight feet long. Select a tree that is straight and without side branches. Every knot in the log will cause you problems later on. The log should not be allowed to dry out. If you cannot split it up immediately, wrap the ends in wet burlap and plastic bags.

Splitting the log is the most strenuous part of basket-making. One person can do it, but if you are new to this type of work, two people will be more efficient. The splitting is best done with metal wedges and a sledgehammer. If you don't have metal wedges, start the split with an ax and continue it with homemade hardwood wedges. Your halved log will lie nicely across two sawhorses, so this is a good time to debark it using a drawknife, hand ax or sheath knife. Allow the bark to remain on portions of the log that will not be used immediately, and wrap these portions in wet burlap and plastic.

The next step is to split the halved log into quarters and then into eighths. Wedges or an ax can be used for this, but an old-fashioned cleaving tool called a froe that was used for making shingles is ideal. If you use an ax, drive it with a wooden mallet, not a metal hammer.

77

You will observe that the narrow end of the wedge-shaped section of wood is darker. This is the heartwood and must be split off using a froe or hand ax. The remaining piece of sapwood is the piece actually used in basket-making.

The pieces of sapwood must now be reduced to the splits used in fashioning a basket. Our favorite tool for doing this is a large, sharp sheath knife. It's a good idea to wear gloves to prevent cuts, splinters or blisters. Your biggest problem will likely be that some of your splits will "run out," that is, the wood fibers will separate in such a way as to allow your knife to run out of wood, leaving you with a short split. When this starts to happen, bend the split over. Oddly enough, this rather drastic action repositions the wood fibers and prevents the "running out."

Remember that you are splitting the oak, not cutting it. The blade used should be sharp, however, because some stray wood fibers must be cut in the process. Chances are you will have some splits that vary in thickness or some with whiskers. These can be worked over with a sharp knife. For weaving, splits should be between 1/16- and 3/16-inch thick and 1/2 to 1 1/4 inches wide. Framing splits should be about 1/4-inch thick and one inch wide.

To start your basket, bend two of the heavier frame pieces into loops and fasten together. Use waxed string or tacks to hold them. If the frame pieces will not bend easily, try soaking them in hot water or scraping them to reduce their thickness. The length of these frame pieces will determine the size of your finished basket. Both rim and handle pieces should be about the same length. A basket roughly 17 inches across has frame pieces 52 inches in length. Frame pieces 42 inches long will make a basket about 13 inches across.

This is how to remove the heartwood from the sapwood with a froe and mallet.

A heavy, sharp knife is the best tool to use in making oak splits.

This partially completed small basket is made entirely of oak splits. The pointed ribs are started by inserting their pointed ends in the original weaving.

The weaving begins at the points where the rim and handle-frame pieces cross, and proceeds toward the middle of the basket. Start weaving with the narrowest and most flexible of your splits, or use some other weaving material. A more flexible material such as twisted grass sometimes makes it easier to start and gives a nice color and texture contrast.

The first weaving will be a simple over-under, going round and round the four fixed pieces of the frame. After weaving about a dozen pieces, you will discover that this process will not allow you to complete the basket. Eight additional ribs are needed in the bottom. These should be made from heavier splits and tapered to a point at each end. Start by inserting one rib into the weaving on each side of the handle. Continue weaving over and under the ribs. After the ribs are added, all weaving is done in the bowl of the basket proper instead of around the handles.

A word should be said about the flexibility of your oak splits. If your weaving splits are about 1/16-inch thick, you will have little trouble. However, when you bend a split back over the rim, you may find that more limberness is desirable. That's done easily by scraping both sides with a sharp knife.

Weaving splits over and under the ribs and back down over the rim gets simpler as you continue toward the middle of the basket. To introduce a new split, just tuck it in a few ribs back and continue weaving. Naturally, longer splits will make a neater basket. When the weaving comes together in the center, be sure you don't leave a space between the splits. It's better to overlap splits for a row than to leave space.

Your basket is essentially finished at this point, but you may want to do two more things. The first is to go round the rim with a thin, narrow split. That dresses up the rim and gives added strength to the basket. If it's important that your basket stands squarely on a flat surface, weave in two splits containing two short legs.

At this point step back and survey your work. You have created a handsome, useful basket from nothing but a log. The amazing lightness and strength of oak splits will make this basket a practical item in the garden as well as an artistic example of a bygone craft.

Warren Asa

Homespun Linen from Flax

For two centuries, flax was one of the main sources of fabric in American clothing; but with the introduction of synthetic material in the early 1920s, interest in natural fibers waned. Now that enthusiasm for homespun fabrics has returned, we are only a step away from homemade linen and linsy-woolsy. Making linen from flax is not much more difficult than making cotton or wool yarn.

Man has grown flax for thousands of years. Mummies in Egyptian tombs are wrapped in fine linen, indeed a much finer linen than we know how to make today. Flax production has been on a decline in our country; none is grown commercially for linen. The plants are used for linseed oil, with the fibers being utilized for cigarette and other fine papers.

Flax seems to do better in cool, dry climates, and today is grown mostly in the more northerly areas: Canada, Russia, and our northern-most Plains States. Acreage in the United States in 1976 was about 1.4 million, down from 1.8 million in 1975, because the current higher wheat prices have lured farmers into shifting land formerly used for flax into wheat. Flax can be grown in almost any state; varieties have flourished in Oregon, Texas and even Georgia. Before 1900, Kentucky and Ohio were the leading producers.

Flax is grown much like wheat, drilled (or broadcast) about an inch deep, two to three pecks per acre. A thick stand will discourage branching and therefore make longer, smoother stalks for longer

While swingling, the worker rests the bunch of stems on the sharp edge of an upright board standing about belt high.

The woody stems surrounding the fibers fall to the ground when struck by the knife.

fibers. It is planted early in the season, and good soils should not need fertilizer. Flax competes poorly with the weeds which extra fertilizer could encourage. Do not plant after sorghum, millet or sudan grass, whose rotting roots may be harmful to the growing flax. CUTHBERT is a new variety of flax outstanding for wilt and rust resistance, but it was bred mainly for seed production. For fiber production, ARNY might be a better variety to try. You can expect at least a ton of straw per acre from which to extract fiber, and usually more. A tenth of an acre would give a hobbyist about all the fiber he or she would want to spin the first time.

Flax grows fairly fast and its blue blossoms begin in June. It keeps on blooming like buckwheat does, but later blooms do not develop mature seeds, and so there is no reason to wait on it to mature. In commercial plantings, when most of the seed is ripe, the crop is cut and swathed, and ripening completed in the swath. If you want to make linen, do not cut the stalks, but pull them up so that you obtain longer fibers.

The flax plants, after having been pulled, are allowed to dry and the seed heads cut or combed out. The stalks are soaked in water or left on the ground exposed to the weather for several weeks to rot the woody stems around the fibers. When the stems have deteriorated, the plants are dried again, and then passed through a tool called a flaxbrake, one bunch at a time.

The flaxbrake is about the size of a sawhorse, which it somewhat resembles. The flax stems are laid across three (usually) wooden boards or bars, and another set of bars, hinged at one end of the sawhorse affair, is lowered or dropped between the fixed lower boards, breaking the flax stems.

The broken stems are scraped or "scutched" away with a swingling knife, which looks like a corn knife, but is made entirely of wood. While swingling, the worker rests the bunch of stems on the sharpened edge of a perpendicular board that measures about an inch thick and six inches across and stands about belt high. The woody stem pieces surrounding the fibers fall to the ground under the onslaught of the swingling knife.

Next the worker passes his handful of fibers through a hetchel (or hacksel) which looks like a large brush, with steel teeth (or combs) spaced widely apart rather than brush fibers. This step, called hackling, straightens the fibers and pulls out all remaining stem pieces. The worker has left in his hand what looks like the end of a horsetail, only much finer and fluffier. When you are watching the process, this appearance of a switch of fibers seems rather sudden and a bit magical. It takes about as long to describe the process as to do it.

The fiber is then spun into yarn—and quite nice yarn, too—that makes very durable clothing. Incidentally, craft historians tell me that flax can be spun on either the smaller flax wheels or the larger wool wheels.

If you are experimenting with flax, you might also like to know that the raw oil pressed from the seeds is much sought after by violin makers to finish the wood of their finest instruments.

"Usually you can get very small amounts of flax seed—a gram or so—free from any of the agricultural experiment stations in the states of Minnesota, North Dakota or South Dakota," says Dr. C. D. Dybing, flax specialist at the University of South Dakota. "Pound or bushel lots can be purchased from the same source, as well as from commercial seed dealers. Ornamental flax seed is available from

The worker next passes his handful of fibers through a large-toothed brush to straighten them and pull out the remaining stem pieces.

The fiber is then spun into yarn that makes very durable clothing. Flax can be spun on either large wool or smaller flax wheels.

horticultural seed suppliers." An all-around source of information on flax and sources of seed is the Flax Development Committee, Flax Institute of the United States, P. O. Box 15049, Minneapolis, Minn. 55415.

SPINNING SUPPLIES

Spinning Wheels
Handcraft House
110 West Esplanade
North Vancouver, BC
Canada

Made-Well Mfg. Co.
Sifton, Manitoba
Canada

C. & G. Rognualdson
R.R.#4
Acton, Ontario
Canada

Wheel Plans
The Unicorn
Box 645
Rockville, Md. 20851

Woodcraft
313 Montvale Ave.
Woburn, Mass. 01801

Books and Equipment
Clewes & Clewes
665 San Pablo Ave.
Pinole, Calif. 94564

Turning Point
1806 Bancroft Way
Berkeley, Calif. 94703

Straw Into Gold
5509 College Ave.
Oakland, Calif. 94618

Whole Earth Truck Store
558 Santa Cruz
Menlo Park, Calif. 94025

Gene Logsdon

A Heavy-Duty Workbench

At the heart of every home workplace should be a sturdy workbench made to hold up under years of use and abuse. The bench we constructed for use at the OGF Workshop is 79 inches long, 26½ inches wide, and stands 38 inches high. With four drawers 23 inches deep, it's a practical design that can be easily adapted to any number of shop layouts and specialized uses. The cost of materials came to $47.

1. Using full 1-inch-thick oak lumber or any hardwood, glue enough boards together to form a width of 26½ inches. While the length of the bench is optional, the one shown here is 79 inches.

2. The six legs are made from 2-inch hardwood, 38 inches long and 3 inches wide. To increase their strength, dado the legs to a depth of $\frac{9}{16}$ inch and to a width of 3 inches, leaving a 7-inch space between dadoes. Then run a router with a $\frac{3}{8}$-inch quarter-round bit along both back edges opposite the dadoed side.

3. The drawer frame is made from 1$\frac{1}{8}$-inch stock. Cut four pieces 74$\frac{3}{8}$ inches long and 3 inches wide. In addition cut two pieces 13 inches by 1$\frac{1}{4}$ inches which will be used for the dividers between the drawers. Dado the four pieces $\frac{9}{16}$-inch deep at the center and 2 inches from either end to accommodate the 3-inch legs. Locate the centers between the legs of the two pieces that will be used for the front and dado to half-depth to fit dividers. Using 1$\frac{1}{2}$-inch #10 wood screws, screw and glue the legs to their proper places and glue the dividers into place.

4. Cut the four end-pieces from 2-inch stock, making them 23$\frac{3}{16}$ inches long and 3 inches wide. Glue, position and fasten with 1$\frac{1}{2}$-inch #10 wood screws. Make sure to drill all pilot holes for screws deep enough to glue in the proper size dowel plugs. From $\frac{3}{4}$-inch pine, saw the two pieces that will fit exactly between the end-pieces; glue and nail. Also from 2-inch stock cut two pieces 3 inches wide and 23$\frac{3}{16}$ inches long. Insert these flush with the top edge of the front and back frame and fasten with 1$\frac{1}{2}$-inch #10 wood screws.

5. With $\frac{3}{4}$-inch by 3-inch pine build a rectangle to fit between the legs. Fasten with 1-inch #10 wood screws 5 inches from the bottom of the legs. Cover this with a piece of $\frac{1}{2}$-inch plywood and you will have a handy shelf, besides adding strength to the workbench.

Nine-sixteenth-inch dadoes, 3 inches wide, make legs extra sturdy.

Drawer slides, below, are 1-inch hardwood with $\frac{1}{2}$-inch by $\frac{1}{2}$-inch rabbets.

6. The drawer slides are made from 1-inch hardwood and have a ½-inch by ½-inch rabbet. One is 4 inches wide and two are 2¾ inches wide with a rabbet on one edge only. From a piece of scrap stock approximately ¾-inch square, cut lengths the width of the drawer slides, two for each slide. Glue and nail these to the bottom edge of the slides, and fasten them to the appropriate places with 1-inch #10 wood screws.
7. The four drawers are made from ¾-inch pine with ¼-inch mahogany plywood bottoms. Cut the following pieces: eight

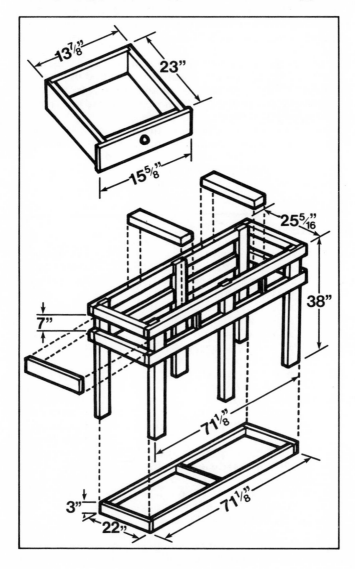

pieces 23 inches by 6⅞ inches; four pieces 13⅞ inches by 6⅞ inches; and four pieces 15⅝ inches by 7⅜ inches. Rabbet one end of the 23-inch pieces ⅜-inch deep and ¾-inch wide, also the two ends of the 15⅝-inch pieces ⅜-inch deep and 1¼ inches wide. Rabbet all pieces along the bottom inside edge ⅜-inch deep and 5⁄16-inch wide to accommodate the drawer bottoms. Be careful to put this rabbet on the same surface as the end rabbets.

8. Next, rabbet the inside top of the drawer fronts ⅜-inch deep and ½-inch wide. Using 1¼-inch finishing nails, glue and nail drawer sides to the back. (For a more polished job, use a ⅜-inch quarter-round bit in router to round off both inside and outside top edges of the drawers.) Cut drawer bottoms to proper size, glue and nail from bottom and attach drawer pulls.

9. Sand all joints smooth. Using a router and quarter-round bit, round all edges on legs, front and sides of frame. Now set the router to approximately one-half depth and round-off the inside edges of the drawer frame.

10. Center the top, making sure the back is flush with the outer edge of the frame. Fasten with 1½-inch #10 wood screws and plug screw holes with dowels. Round off the top edge with router and sand. Several coats of a dull finish polyurethane varnish will protect the bench from stains.

Materials

Quantity	Size and Description	Purpose
1	1″x26½″x79″ glued hardwood	bench top
4	1″x23³⁄16″x2¾″ hardwood	drawer slide
1	1″x23³⁄16″x4″ hardwood	drawer slide
8	¾″x23″x6⅞″ pine	drawer slide
4	¾″x13⅞″x6⅞″ pine	drawer back
4	¾″x15⅝″x7⅜″ pine	drawer front
2	¾″x71⅛″x3″ pine	bottom shelf frame
2	¾″x22″x3″ pine	bottom shelf frame
1	¾″x20½″x3″ pine	bottom shelf frame
2	¾″x25⁵⁄16″x7″ pine	side panel
10	¾″x¾″x3″ pine	gluing blocks for slides
4	1⅛″x74⅜″x3″ pine or hardwood	front and back frame
2	1⅛″x13″x1¼″ pine or hardwood	drawer dividers
6	2″x38″x3″ hardwood	legs
4	2″x23³⁄16″x3″ hardwood	frame ends
2	2″x23³⁄16″x3″ hardwood	top supports
4	¼″x22⅝″x13⅞″ plywood	drawer bottoms
1	½″x71⅛″x22″ plywood	shelf

Note: Also needed are a wood dowel for screw holes, #10 (1½″ and 1″) wood screws, knobs, glue, finishing nails and finishing materials.

A Homemade Hive

Getting started in beekeeping, even on a small scale, can be an expensive proposition. The bees themselves aren't that costly, but there is a lot of equipment, ranging from hives to veils and smokers to extractors, that is necessary. The modern beehive consists of a brood body, with a removable top and a separate bottom. The brood body is a 9⅝-inch-deep frame without top or bottom, which holds ten comb frames. The beekeeper stacks additional hive bodies—either deep supers of the same size as the brood body or smaller ones called shallow supers—atop the brood chamber, filling these bodies with ten frames each. The queen will fill the brood chamber's combs with eggs; the worker bees will fill the supers' combs with honey. A certain amount of honey will be needed by the bees to see them through the winter, but most years, they'll make and store far more than they need; the beekeeper harvests this excess.

The biggest single expense in beekeeping is the hive. Although good hives are constructed to very exacting standards, there's no good reason why a competent home handyman can't make his own hive components.

The most important part is getting all the dimensions exactly right.

Dimensions are critical because of what is known as bee space. The commonly accepted bee space is 5/16 inch, but it ranges from ¼ inch to ⅜ inch. Bees will plug up any space or hole smaller than 3/16 inch with a tough, sticky substance called propolis. In a space larger than ⅜ inch, the bees will build comb. Before the proper size of the bee space was figured out, beekeeping was a sticky proposition, because the bees would weld all the comb frames together and to the body with propolis and comb. The individually movable frame is a vital—more than convenient—part of modern beekeeping.

A circular saw, a hammer, and a paintbrush are the only tools necessary to make your own supers and hive bodies. You'll also need some cement-coated or galvanized 7d nails and a quart of acrylic exterior paint for ten to twelve supers. Different colors of paint are best for a large number of hives to help the bees distinguish their hive from others, but if you have only a few hives, one color, usually white, will do fine.

Each hive body (or deep super) requires a 6-foot length of 1x12 lumber. This length is sufficient for one deep super plus some useful leftovers. Knots are all right in bee super lumber if they are strongly attached. It's good practice to buy enough lumber for at least four supers per colony.

BROOD CHAMBER (DEEP SUPER)

Construction

1. Rip a 6-foot 1x12 to an actual width of 9⅝ inches. Cut the board into four pieces: two side pieces 19⅞ inches long and two end-pieces 15½ inches long.

2. The body will be assembled using a rabbet joint, with the rabbets cut in the butt ends of the sides. The rabbet should be half the thickness of the stock deep, ⅜ inch, and the width of the stock wide, ¾ inch. For the best finish, the rabbets should be partially stopped, since the top edge of the ends must be rabbeted to accept the comb frames. Since this latter rabbet will be the same size—⅜-inch wide and ¾-inch deep—stop the former rabbets ¾ inch from the top edge of the sides and rabbet that small portion only ⅜-inch wide.

3. Cut a ¾-inch-wide by ⅜-inch-deep rabbet along the top edge of the end-pieces.

4. Cut a ½-inch-deep finger grip into each piece of the body. The grips should be about 5 inches long and should be centered in each piece, about 3 inches below and parallel to the top edge. An option would be to nail a 5-inch length of 1x1 in the same position for a grip.

5. Using five 8d cement-coated or galvanized box nails and a bit of waterproof glue at each joint, fasten the sides and ends together.

6. Cut two 14¾-inch lengths of 1-inch-wide galvanized sheet metal or aluminum and tack them to the ends along the rabbets for the comb frames. These strips should project ⅛ inch above the bottom of the rabbet. Their purpose is to make the removal of the frames much easier. Remember that the amount the strips project above the bottom surface of the rabbet is critical, because if they project less than ⅛ inch, the bee space will be too big, and if they project more than ¼ inch, the bee space will be too small.

7. Paint the entire outside of the body with two or more heavy coats of acrylic paint. A light color will help keep the hive cooler in summer. It is not necessary to paint the inside of the body.

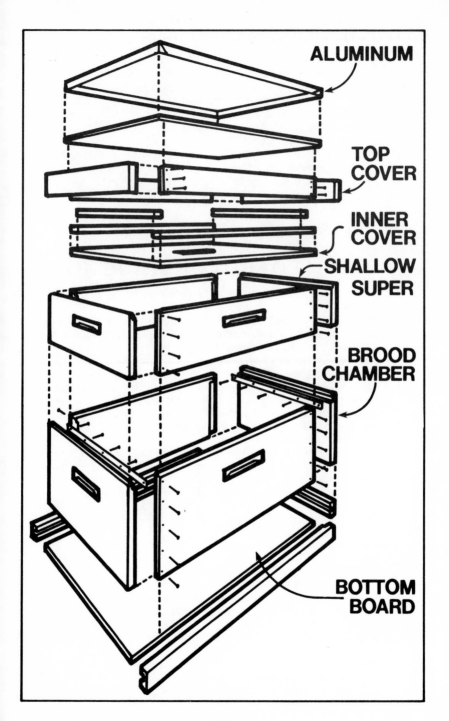

ALUMINUM

TOP COVER

INNER COVER

SHALLOW SUPER

BROOD CHAMBER

BOTTOM BOARD

Materials (for brood chamber)

Wood
> 1 pc. 1x12x6' or
>> Sides: 2 pcs. ¾" by 9⅝" by 19⅞"
>> Ends: 2 pcs. ¾" by 9⅝" by 15½"

Hardware
> 8d cement-coated box nails
> Waterproof glue
> 1 pc. 1" by 29½", ¹⁄₃₂" galvanized sheet metal or Frame
>> support strips:
>> 2 pcs. 1" by 14¾"
> Tacks
> Acrylic paint

BOTTOM BOARD CONSTRUCTION

1. Cut a piece of ⅜-inch exterior plywood 15½ inches by 21¾ inches.
2. Rip nominal 1-inch material to an actual width of 1⅝ inches. If you have made a super, use the strips ripped from the 1x12 or 1x8 used to make the super for this purpose. Cut the ¾-inch by 1⅝-inch strip into two pieces 22⅛ inches long and one piece 15½ inches long.
3. Rip a ⅜-inch-wide by ⅜-inch-deep dado the full length of each piece in a board face, locating its center ⁹⁄₁₆ inch from the bottom edge. Cut a ¾-inch-wide by ⅜-inch-deep rabbet in one butt end of each of the long pieces. The rabbet should be in the same face as the dado.
4. Slip the frame pieces over the edges of the plywood, as shown, and secure with a bit of waterproof glue and 6d cement-coated box nails.
5. Paint the assembled bottom board with acrylic paint.

Materials (for bottom board)

Wood
> 1-2' sq. sht. ⅜" ext. plywood or
>> Bottom: 1 pc. 15½" by 21¾"
>> Side Frames: 2 pcs. ¾" by 1⅝" by 22⅛" (use waste strips ripped in making supers)
>> End Frame: 1 pc. ¾" by 1⅝" by 15½" (use waste strips ripped in supers)

Hardware
> Waterproof glue
> 6d cement-coated box nails
> Acrylic paint

INNER COVER CONSTRUCTION

1. Cut a 19⅞-inch by 16¼-inch piece of ⅜-inch exterior plywood.
2. Rip a 6-foot strip of the waste from construction of a super to an actual width of ⁵⁄₁₆ inch. Cut this strip into two pieces 19⅞ inches long and two strips 14¾ inches long.
3. Using waterproof glue, attach the strips around the top of the plywood cover, flush with the edges.
4. Using a keyhole saw, cut a hole 1⅛ inches wide and 3¾ inches long in the center of the cover.

Materials (for inner cover)

Wood
1-2′ sq. sht. ⅜″ ext. plywood or
    Cover: 1 pc. 19⅞″ by 16¼″
    Frame Sides: 2 pcs. ¾″ by ⁵⁄₁₆″ by 19⅞″
    Frame Ends: 2 pcs. ¾″ by ⁵⁄₁₆″ by 14¾″ (use waste strips from super construction)

Hardware
Waterproof glue

TOP COVER CONSTRUCTION

1. From 1x2 material, cut two 21¾-inch lengths and two 16½-inch lengths. From ½-inch exterior plywood, cut a piece 18 inches by 21¾ inches.
2. Using 8d cement-coated box nails, nail the 1x2's together, forming a frame 18 inches by 21¾ inches. Using 6d cement-coated box nails, nail the plywood to the top of the frame.
3. Cut a piece of galvanized sheet metal or aluminum 19½ inches by 23¼ inches. Use this metal to cover the wooden top cover, lapping the metal over the sides and ends of the cover at least ⅝ inch to ¾ inch to provide a watertight seal. Use ½-inch tacks to attach the metal to the cover.
4. Paint the cover with acrylic paint.

Materials (for top cover)

Wood
1 pc. 1x2x8′ or
    Frame Sides: 2 pcs. 1x2 by 21¾″
    Frame Ends: 2 pcs. 1x2 by 16½″
1-2′ sq. sht. ½″ ext. plywood or
    Top: 1 pc. 18″ by 21¾″

Hardware
>
> 8d cement-coated box nails
> 6d cement-coated box nails
> 1 pc. 19½″ by 23¼″, ⅟₃₂″ galvanized sheet metal
> ½″ tacks
> Acrylic paint

SHALLOW SUPER CONSTRUCTION

The shallow super is constructed in the same fashion as the brood chamber. However, use a 1x8 instead of a 1x12, and rip it to an actual width of $5^{11}/_{16}$ inches. Cut it into the same length pieces, rabbet them in the same fashion, assemble them, install the frame support strips, and paint.

Materials (for shallow super)

Wood
>
> 1 pc. 1x8x6′ or
>> Sides: 2 pcs. ¾″ by $5^{11}/_{16}$″ by 19⅞″
>> Ends: 2 pcs. ¾″ by $5^{11}/_{16}$″ by 15½″

Hardware
>
> 8d cement-coated box nails
> Waterproof glue
> 1 pc. 1″ by 29½″, ⅟₃₂″ galvanized sheet metal
>> or Frame Support Strips: 2 pcs. 1″ by 14¾″
> Tacks
> Acrylic paint

Build a Honey Extractor (For Under $30)

The honey extractor has revolutionized beekeeping since the turn of this century. With its use, honeycombs can be emptied and then put back with the bees to be used over again. That brings a considerable saving in time and labor, since the bees do not have to build new comb each time.

Most honey extractors operate on the concept of centrifugal force. The machine whirls combs of honey around and around at a high rate of speed. The honey is thrown out and away from the comb.

There are many extractor designs; most are available from beekeeping supply houses. They normally range from $100 upwards to about $500.

Probably the most efficient design is the radial extractor. The frames of honeycomb are placed vertically into holders or "baskets" which radiate out from a central axle, much like the spokes of a wheel. The advantage of this system is that both sides of the comb are emptied without having to stop the machine and turn the comb around. Also, very few combs break or are deformed with this design.

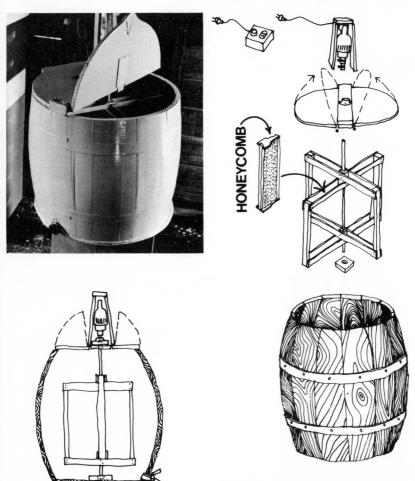

Expanded view of barrel and working parts shows the drill is mounted on a crosspiece and the vertical shaft.

93

The comb must be uncapped before being put into the extractor. A hot knife will easily slice through the thin wax cappings.

We built the very serviceable extractor pictured here mostly from an old wooden barrel, a few stocks of wood, and a ¼-inch power hand drill. The drill turns the shaft and "baskets" of the extractor. Its speed must be regulated and increased slowly. For this purpose, a common dimmer switch or rheostat must be used, or you must use a variable-speed drill.

If a barrel is not available, a large wooden box can be made to serve in its place. Basically it acts as a shield for the flying honey and as a foundation to mount the other parts. The liquid honey will run down the side of this "tank" and should flow out of a hole near the bottom and into a waiting bucket.

Our extractor is a four-frame model. The baskets which hold the honeycomb frames are attached to a rotating shaft. The shaft's lower bearing is simply a hardwood block with a hole the same diameter of the shaft drilled partway through. This wooden block is nailed into the bottom-center of the barrel. The shaft rests in this socket.

The drill is mounted on a 2x4 crosspiece. The shaft passes up through a hole bored in this crosspiece and is coupled securely to the chuck on the drill.

A hinged cover will protect the room from flying droplets of honey. After the machine is loaded with honeycombs, care must be made not to start the extractor spinning too quickly. A slow increase in speed will result in fewer, if any, broken combs.

Terry Domico

Build This Energy-Free Solar Dryer

Solar drying of fruits and vegetables follows the same reasoning as gardening organically. It is the oldest, simplest and most natural way of preserving our food. When we compare solar drying to other methods of preservation, we find even more reasons for its viability. Much, if not all, of the energy gained by foods produced organically is lost when methods of preservation such as canning or freezing are employed. The energy requirements encountered in producing canning jars and their non-reusable lids, as well as freezers and their

The inventor of the solar dryer, Leandre Poisson, checks the progress of drying vegetables at his New Hampshire home with an early model of the dryer.

The latest versions have more drying racks to increase the capacity. Depending on what size drum is used, the unit can have as many as five drying trays.

storage containers, must be considered a minus. The energies required to process the jars and to power the freezers are an even greater minus. In a very short time, the energy that you gained from the sun is lost to the energy required to preserve and maintain the food.

The solar dehydrators that people are most familiar with look somewhat like a cold frame with ventilation holes in their sides and trays to hold food under a piece of glass. Another type looks like a cookie sheet with cheesecloth spread over the food. Both of these work fairly well in sunny, dry areas, but they barely function in temperate, damp regions.

Another big disadvantage of these dryers is that in order to dehydrate, the food must be exposed to direct sunlight. This causes food pieces to heat up to unregulated internal temperatures, resulting in caramelized and crusted pieces that are unevenly dried. The direct exposure also destroys color, vitamins and flavor. A final drawback to the serious gardener with these systems is their small size, or incapacity to dry large quantities evenly at once.

The ideal conditions needed for dehydrating are: being out of direct sunlight; not heating the food, but moving heated air across the food at a constant rate, thereby lifting the moisture off and carrying it out of the dehydrator; and maintaining a temperature range of 95 to 100 degrees F. Until now it has been possible to achieve these conditions only by using heat sources other than direct sunlight. Sources such as electric heat elements, with their necessary air-circulating fans, top-of-the-stove dehydrators, and kitchen ovens all have worked, but with each a new energy price must be paid.

The "Solar Survival Dehydrator," invented and designed by Leandre Poisson, meets all the requirements for drying, and does it only with solar energy. His dehydrator keeps food out of direct sunlight, dries by moving warm air around the food, and holds at about 110 degrees F on an average sunny, summer day.

The dryer consists of a cutout 55-gallon drum placed inside a plywood and "Sun-Lite" plastic covering. As shown in the diagram, the curved solar collector enables the unit to receive even exposure to the sun all day long when properly positioned. The sun heats the air between the two layers of plastic, and natural convection forces it down and into the drying chamber built inside the 55-gallon drum. Natural convection then pulls the heated air up and through the drying chamber and out the vents at the top of the unit. To enable the unit to be used year-round, and even inside, light bulbs may be placed at the bottom of the unit to produce heat to continue the drying process in the absence of sunlight.

In the past two years of testing, the unit has performed extremely well, reaching and holding 110 degrees F on overcast days, and holding 110 on extremely sunny days by opening all vents.

The Poissons have devised several additional uses for the dryer. It has proven well suited for such diverse duties as extracting honey, drying flowers, hatching chicken eggs, and incubating tempeh.

Depending on how much of your materials you have to buy, a dryer could be built for $35 to $50 per unit. Plans for complete construction and use of the unit are available for $6 from Leandre Poisson, Solar Survival, Box 118, Harrisville, N.H. 03450.

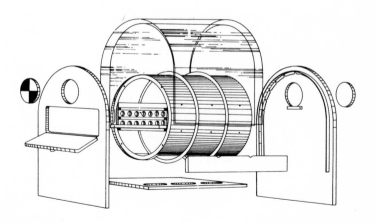

The solar dryer is designed to be made at home, and calls for no special tools or abilities.

Insulating Shutters That Save Energy

Windows are a mixed blessing. On sunny winter days the solar gain through the windows is often enough to turn off the thermostat. At sunset, however, we can virtually hear the oil running into the furnace to replace the heat escaping through the same windows. In the northern United States, most windows lose more heat than they gain. Only south-facing, double-glazed windows gain more heat than they lose.

This has led some designers to believe that the best house is one with no windows at all! I disagree. The psychological benefits of windows make it imperative that we find a better solution.

What we need is a window which effectively turns into a wall at night. There are dozens of ingenious schemes in the marketplace which effect this transformation, ranging from aluminized-fabric shades to motorized panels. I have experimented with a number of these approaches, but had not found one that satisfied all of the design criteria:

- high thermal R-factor
- vapor resistance to prevent window icing
- convenient to operate
- attractive
- adaptable to existing windows
- low cost
- long life
- simple

Until now. Through some fortuitous coming together of time and function, the student owner-builders and teachers of Cornerstones Building School have evolved an insulating shutter so simple, so effective and so attractive that one's first thought is, "Eureka!"

The shutter is made of two sheets of Thermoply, a high density cardboard, covered with either a low emissivity foil or a white plastic film. These are separated by four sticks of wood, then covered with the fabric of your choice and hinged to the inside of the window frame. The construction requires only a handsaw, screwdriver, utility knife, scissors and a staple gun. The cost of materials averages 50 cents per square foot plus fabric.

The shutter works by trapping dead air on four surfaces; two outside and two inside. In addition, three of the surfaces are highly reflective to heat radiation. A measure of resistance to heat loss, through a wall or window, is the thermal resistance, called "R." The R value of a single-glazed window is one, a double-glazed window is two, and a double-glazed window plus shutter is eight. By using this shutter, the heat loss of a typical double-glazed window is four times less and a single-glazed window is seven times less!

Table 1 shows the annual heat lost (expressed in gallons of oil) by typical single-glazed and double-glazed windows before and after the installation of the shutters. Even though all windows lose heat continually, most windows gain some solar heat during the day. The important figure is the difference between the loss and the gain. While the shutters can't perform the impossible trick of converting the north side losers to winners, they sure can reduce the fuel bill.

TABLE 1

NET HEAT GAIN (+) or loss (-) for a typical 10-square-foot window in Augusta, Maine, 44° lat., 8,000 heating degree days. (Expressed in gallons of oil/year)

	Single-Glazed	Double-Glazed*	Single-Glazed Plus Shutter	Double-Glazed Plus Shutter
Net Loss (-)				
Net Gain (+)				
North Window	-17.5 Gal.	-8.1 Gal.	-6.5 Gal.	-3.3 Gal.
South Window	- 3.6 Gal.	+4.4 Gal.	+7.4 Gal.	+9.2 Gal.

*Double-Glazed includes either thermopane or storm window.

Construction

1. Measure the height (h) and width (w) from inside to inside of the present window trim.
2. Cut, with a utility knife and straightedge, four pieces of Thermoply so that, when two are placed side by side, they measure (h—⅜ inch) X (w—¼ inch).
3. Cut eight pieces of ¾-inch pine to form two rectangles of the same dimensions as the Thermoply. The width of the pine is not critical, but ½ inch is recommended.
4. Fasten Thermoply to both sides of the pine frames using B. F. Goodrich PL 200 mastic and staples.
5. Fasten two sets of ¾-by-1½-inch loose-pin hinges about 6 inches from the top and bottom of each shutter without cutting into the wood.

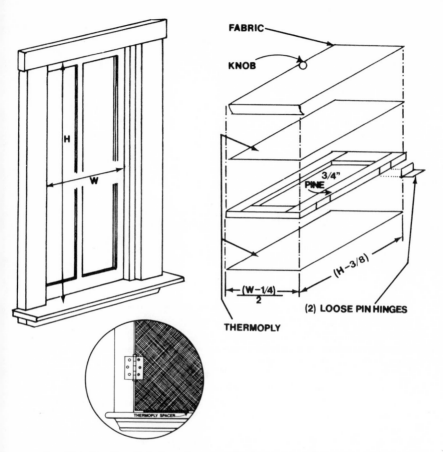

6. Staple the fabric of your choice around the edge of each shutter, cutting away from the hinges.
7. Staple a weatherstrip (old-fashioned felt works well) to the hinge edge of each shutter. Cut away from the hinge locations.
8. Place a scrap piece of Thermoply under each shutter while holding in place and mark location of the hinge against the window trim.
9. Open the shutter and fasten the hinges to the window trim.
10. Nail a ¾-by-1-inch strip of pine with a weatherstrip to the windowsill so that the shutters close tightly against it.
11. The shutter pair should be slightly too wide for the space so that moderate force is required to close. If not snug enough, add a weatherstrip to the mating edge of one. If they don't remain closed, install a cabinet "bullet catch" at the bottom of one of the shutters.
12. As a final touch, add a pair of little porcelain knobs so that your "wall" can be turned back into a window at sunrise!

Charles G. Wing

Greywater Irrigation Systems

When it comes to reusing water from your house, there is some good news, and some bad news. First the good news: it is possible to reuse every drop of water that comes into your house, safely. Now for the bad news: it is illegal to do so.

The illegalities have been readily overlooked by health officials throughout the Far West during the recent drought, so you didn't have to worry if you live there. If you live in an area that isn't having a drought, but your well water is limited, or you just don't like the idea of wasting a lot of water, your greywater utilization project will have to be done without official sanction.

In the lexicon of the plumbing world, greywater is known as any water that is used in the home for any use except flushing toilets. Water from toilets is designated as black water, in honor of its higher bacteria content and disease potential. Home treatment of black water is a risky business, and you should not get involved with it. If you want to stop wasting fresh water for flushing a toilet, fill the toilet manually with collected greywater and flush with that. You can realize a substantial savings of water by installing water-saving devices, turning off the water supply to the toilet, and using the collected greywater for flushing.

The amount of usable greywater in a house can be substantial. Of the 600 gallons of water used daily by the average California household (pre-drought), about one-third could be reclaimed for use in the garden.

According to research done at Ecology Action of the Midpeninsula, in Palo Alto, California, 20 gallons of water a day will support 100 square feet of intensively grown vegetables. Thus, the average greywater flow from a home should be able to support almost 1,000 square feet of vegetables—more than a family of four could eat.

However, all greywater is not equal or capturable for possible use.

100

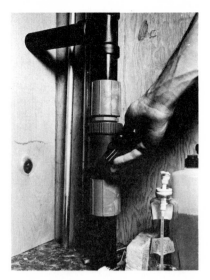

If you disconnect the drain and place buckets under the sink, be sure to cap the disconnected drain.

If you install an alternative system, place the switching valves below the existing drain junctions.

Unfortunately, the more you conserve water in the home, the more concentrated the pollutants in greywater become, and the more caution you must use. Although individual homes will vary, graywater experts agree that the best sources of usable greywater are: bathroom tub and sink, followed by the washing machine, dishwasher and, lastly, the kitchen sink.

Since the kitchen is the source of most strong chemical cleaners, grease, food scraps and other problem-causers, we think it is best to capture kitchen sink water separately to use for toilet flushing, and concentrate your greywater efforts on the bathroom and laundry.

Methods used to capture greywater will be as different as the individual homes' plumbing systems. What works well in one home won't work in another. However, there are some general guidelines we can offer.

If you simply disconnect the drain and place buckets under the sink, be sure to cap the disconnected drain, as black water is still circulating in the system and has odor- and disease-causing potential. If you install an alternative plumbing system, place the switching valves below the existing drain junctions, so any blockage will back up and go into the existing system. Be absolutely sure you have completely segregated greywater from black water. When you have your system all set up, flush a container of septic tank dye used for finding drain fields down the toilet, and then use your greywater system to see if you get any of the dye in your reusable water. If you do, your system has a leak and you're getting black water in it.

Use shut-off valves and piping wherever possible. If you decide to just catch the water in buckets and carry it to the garden, remember a gallon of water weighs 8½ pounds, and five gallons weigh 42½ pounds.

Greywater use in the garden may be in the spotlight because of the recent drought, but the principles are certainly valid over the long haul, so make your system permanent where you can. Even if there is plenty of water, reuse will only lower your water bill, so view your system as a small investment in your gardening future.

The methods of reusing greywater presented here are only for short-term use. If you wish to set up your own permanent treatment system for reuse of water, it can get quite involved.

Once you've got your capture system, you have to decide if you will be storing the water, or routing it directly to the garden. Storage always carries the risk of the system going septic and having odors, but it also has some advantages. Storing all the water together allows for relatively pure water to be mixed with relatively polluted water to dilute the pollutant. Most experts agree a short-term storage system can act as a buffer and is desirable. Such a storage system can consist of a garbage can or 55-gallon drum, with a slow drain out the bottom. It has to store the water for only a short period of time, to allow hot water to cool, or for the rinse cycle to mix with the wash cycle of a clothes

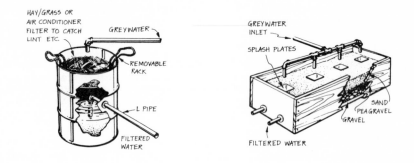

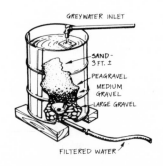

washer. If you set up short-term storage, it should be screened from insects, and the drain inspected frequently. An overflow hose should also be connected near the top of the tank to drain excess into the standard plumbing system when your tank is full or during surges.

After the question of storage, attention next turns to the need to filter greywater. If you will be using the water through a trickle system, you probably will need some type of filter to prevent the small irrigating openings from becoming clogged. If you are merely running the water straight into the garden by hose, you can get by with cloth bags tied to the end of each hose to catch anything that would form a scum blanket on the soil. The bags should be cleaned and changed every week.

There are many things that will affect the overall quality of the greywater you use. If you have a water softener, disconnect it during the months you will be reusing your greywater, as the salts in the softened water will harm soil aggregation, leading to compaction of clay soils.

Do not use any cleaning products containing boron, as rather small excess amounts of this necessary plant nutrient become toxic and will kill plants. Generally, soaps are less harmful than detergents. Use gentle soaps, such as soap flakes, and stay away from detergents and those including lanolin, perfumes, and other chemicals. Do not use any detergent that contains ABS, as it is a plant killer. Biodegradable detergents do not contain ABS and are much preferred to detergents that are not biodegradable. Low-phosphate detergents are preferable.

You may use bleach in limited amounts, but it is best avoided. If you have a short-term storage tank, the effect of bleach will be diluted by rinse waters and will be more tolerable.

Do not allow any chemical cleaners that cannot be used in contact with your skin, to get into your greywater system. From time to time, run a few gallons of boiling water through the greywater capture system (but not directly into the garden) to clean everything out.

Once you have your water captured, it is relatively easy to use it in the garden for flood irrigation. Remember to disperse the water around the garden freely, to avoid any potential localization or buildup of harmful ingredients. Do not spray with greywater, but apply it to the soil directly. Do not use it on delicate seedlings or the restricted root zones of potted plants. Do not use unfiltered greywater in drip or trickle irrigation systems.

Because of the salts in greywater, do not use it on acid-loving plants. Avoid using greywater on crops to be eaten raw, like lettuce and carrots. Root crops will tend to accumulate pollutants in greywater, so be sure to flush the ground in all parts of your garden with irrigation of fresh water on a regular, rotating basis.

Lastly, use greywater on fruit trees and ornamentals if you have any second thoughts about its use in the garden.

Greywater is a resource produced by your household, just as manure is a resource produced by livestock. You must use it carefully, and it requires a little daily or weekly maintenance. During a time of severe water shortage, greywater can make the difference between a successful garden and an empty patch of dusty soil where the garden used to be.

A Pedal-Powered Grain Mill

As the summer's wheat harvest rolled in, everyone's culinary imagination soared at the School of Homesteading in Bangor, Michigan. Various ideas on breads, rolls and pastries began evolving around the flour output of a hand-operated mill. It took but a few days of hand grinding during a Michigan summer to discourage the most dedicated homesteader. Bread-rationing steps were taken, accompanied by such signs in the bread drawer: "EAT NOW, NONE TOMORROW."

Discussions at the dinner table began centering around the drudgery of milling adequate amounts of flour for 15-plus people. Ideas with scheduling were discussed, but it was during one brainstorm period that a bicycle gearing attachment with grinder was suggested. The grinder would be placed ahead of the rider to assure ease of monitoring.

Scrap bicycle parts were gathered to build a solid bicycle wheat grinder, for consistent wheat output with the minimum exertion. The experiment took several weeks to build and to adjust the "bugs" out of the system. A sprocket was attached to the mill's shaft, linked by a chain to the main sprocket. An inverted chicken waterer doubled as a handlebar-mounted wheat hopper and book rest.

Appetites swelled with the increased exercise and bread availability. The wheat-grinding task became a much more favorable chore. Any difficulties that arose resulted mainly from the poor upright riding position and lack of a steady flywheel action. When one is riding a bicycle, the mass of the rider *is* the flywheel.

These problems were alleviated by building a more refined bicycle grinder, based on lessons learned from the first venture. A used 10-speed frame with "dropped" handlebars, narrow saddle, and pedals with toe clips placed the rider in a much more efficient pedaling position. The double chainwheel of the bicycle allowed one chain to go forward to the grinder and another chainwheel to accept the rear-mounted flywheel. The flywheel is a water-filled tire with the

A Quaker City mill can be easily adapted to a stripped bicycle wheat grinder.

freewheel welded to the hub. You don't want the flywheel to freewheel, which would negate any useful transfer of power. As one pedals the wheat into flour, excess flywheel power smooths out the grinder's jerkiness. Your momentum is not interrupted at each dead spot on the stroke. Even a better book rest is being added to hold a wider range of books while riding toward those biscuits!

While constructing the refined grinder, horizons brightened with suggestions to adapt the bicycle/flywheel combination to our homestead chores. Why not attach a unit to the wheat cleaner? For that matter, why not put some mileage into delicious home-churned butter? A standard butter churn purchased at an auction ought to fit the bill nicely after some modifications.

Applications of homestead bicycle technology are endless when one realizes the relative efficiency of the human body in converting solar energy to mechanical work. The following publications: *Energy & Equity* by Ivan Illich and "Bicycle Technology" in *Scientific American*, March 1973, are considered by some to be requisite reading to anyone serious about bicycle technology. The suggested adaptations are endless: a friend of mine has built a three-wheeled rickshaw to carry passengers or tools and supplies while going about his daily work.

For those who are "growing their own," the benefits of the reduced prices and increased nutrition may also include finding out that the undertaking involves a wee bit more labor. Maybe there's some adaptive bicycle technology in your homestead's future?

Jim Burgel

105

And Another . . . Pedal-Powered Grain Mill

Saving energy is an on-going job for Dwayne and Fay Knox. Their pedal-powered grain mill is just one of the energy-saving and labor-saving devices they have built for themselves and their friends who share a 40-acre homestead deep in the Ozark Mountains.

The Knoxes work and play on their place, which was once an old farm. They garden organically, getting most of the food they eat from their garden. Even in the cold of winter, they are able to eat greens and root crops straight from the good earth.

While still in Texas, the Knoxes began to locate good, used tools and equipment for the move to their small farm. Garage sales were a main source of many tools and some of the parts for their human-powered mill. When they arrived at their homestead, they already had much of what they needed. They also brought their newly built bicycle-mill. Making it took many modifications, since they had no pattern to follow, but with help from friends they were able to get it to work. They admit that "it still isn't perfected," but it does the job.

Basically, what the Knoxes did was to take an old bicycle frame and weld a few pieces of pipe to it, making it self-supporting. By putting legs out in front of the handlebars, they were able to balance the rig nicely. A regular hand-crank grain mill was then fastened to a welded piece of angle iron located below the handlebars. To power the mill, they use a 40-tooth sprocket at the pedals and a 52-tooth sprocket at the mill. The recycled 52-tooth sprocket came from the front derailleur of a 10-speed bicycle, and the other came with the frame. A regular bicycle chain lengthened to fit is the only other part.

Bolted to the larger sprocket is a standard pipe flange with an opening large enough to fit the shaft of the mill. At first the mill was fitted to the opening of the flange with molten brass poured around it to give a tight fit. That didn't work well, as the brass flaked out and gave way. Another method would be to weld the socket from the hand crank of the mill right to the sprocket, but the original crank was unusable. Now the Knoxes are going to weld a large nut to the shaft of the mill,

106

The Knoxes welded pieces of pipe to an old bicycle frame and attached a hand-crank grain mill below the handle bars.

then bolt the sprocket on. This final modification should hold the sprocket firmly to the shaft.

Grinding is much less work for the legs than for the arms say Dwayne and Fay, but "it's still a steep hill." They lighten the load by feeding harder grains like wheat into the mill slowly. Corn grinds easily, as do other soft seeds and grains, most of which are turned into flour with one grinding. Another project they recently completed is a large metal frame utility cart. It has a big bed and—you guessed it— bicycle wheels.

Joel and Sherri Davidson

The Davidsons edit the newsletter, Living in the Ozarks, *from their homestead in Pettigrew, Arkansas.*

Getting Started with Wind Power

*Is there a windmill in your future? Clean, quiet
and infinitely renewable wind power has
become a realistic alternative for a growing
number of enthusiasts around the country.*

Wind. It comes; it goes. For most of us wind is a commonplace, a
passing turbulence, not much to notice save when it grabs a hat or
otherwise swoops our way. There is a small and growing group of
people, however, for whom wind is an important event: when the wind
blows for them it's also making electricity. For a variety of reasons
these people have sought the energy of the wind to supply their own
energy needs through the use of wind powered generators.

Paul and Sally Taylor's Australian-made "Dunlite" wind generator
has been operating for almost a year. The Taylors, along with Baggins
the hound, horses, ducks and cats, live on six acres of gently rising
pastureland in an area known as Hessel, a bit east of Sebastopol,
California. They came to Sonoma County from British Columbia,
where Paul was a dentist; now he practices in Cotati.

Coming into Hessel, it is evident that the wind has been working for
many years. Old water-pumping windmills like the "Aermotor" can
be seen here and there, some near familiar water towers. Partway up
the Taylor's drive stands one of these water-pumpers. It's another way
they are using the wind. Paul had it installed over a shallow well, an
old mill put to use again.

At the house the rise tops out and just away from it sits the Dunlite
atop a metal tripod-tower some 25 feet high. When a breeze picks up,
the three-blade propeller silently starts with it, turning gears that step
up the rpm's to the generator behind. At around 7 mph wind speed, the
generator is turning fast enough to deliver useful DC power to the
house or to the storage batteries for times of no wind. With wind power,
power storage is critical since the raw material is so highly inconsis-
tent. So far, batteries, though not highly efficient, are the best solution
for small-scale operations like power for homes. Awaiting further
development is a way of using a spinning flywheel to store the wind's

energy as kinetic energy and then to be drawn out again for use as electricity.

In a shed beneath the Taylor's wind generator are ten 12-volt truck batteries and the voltage regulator control panel. This setup gives them a normal 120-volt current with considerable storage capacity. Paul figures that, fully charged, the batteries could deliver full power for five to seven days of no wind, depending on the load demanded.

Paul is fairly satisfied with the performance of the Dunlite. "We're doing all our lights and some small appliances on wind power. When it's really blowing outside we can hook in the washer. We're very careful with our electricity." Since the generator doesn't supply enough electricity for all their needs, the Taylor's home is still tied in with PG&E power. But it is the feeling of being producer, manager and consumer of their own energy, relatively independent of the power giants, that has drawn Paul and Sally to wind power.

The Dunlite is rated to produce 2,000-2,750 watts of power at its peak, which means a wind of 25 mph. With adequate wind and storage capacity, this is enough for an average household's consumption, save for heavy loads like cooking and heating. Proper site selection is vital. Wind generators are not practical everywhere on the landscape and so are not for all homeowners seeking an alternative energy supply. One way this geographical limitation of wind power could be lessened would be the widespread adoption of what is being called "the reverse meter" principle, wherein a homeowner could put power from the wind back into the public system and thereby reduce his bill. The power companies would in effect be buying electricity from the individual producer, who would still be able to use as much electricity as needed.

Yet even without economic incentives of this sort, the grass roots wind power movement is growing, perhaps faster than the machines involved. Domestic commercial production of wind generators is still at a very early stage. As yet there is only one complete unit made in this country, the "Windcharger" by Dyna Technology, rated at one-tenth the output of the Dunlite. Other systems available here come from Switzerland and France. The Swiss "Electro" wind generators range in output from .8-6 kw (one kilowatt equals 1,000 watts) and in cost up to $6,000. These machines are sold here in the West by the Real Gas & Electric Company of Guerneville, California. Several years ago, Solomon Kagen purchased a Dunlite for his ranch and became so taken by the idea of wind power, that he founded RG&E to make complete wind generator systems and their installation more easily available to the public.

Another firm in Texas is distributing a French version, the "Aerowatt" in models rated up to 4 kw. They are described by Automatic Power of Houston as "highly reliable and efficient, but expensive." Four kilowatts of Aerowatt run over $20,000.

What is sorely needed is the beginning of production in this country to lower the initial cost and to make available an array of designs to meet varying environmental and energy needs. This seems certain to happen as the cost/output ratios of other energy systems continue to rise, making the wind a more economical and feasible energy source.

The surge of interest in owning wind generators has been accompanied by an encouraging increase in research and development. Coming out are kits and all manner of do-it-yourself plans; some aim at economy, some for greater efficiency. Prototypes are appearing everywhere in industry, in our universities, and among independent inventors.

High up on Sonoma Mountain Road near Santa Rosa sits a wind generator atop a short tower made of 4x4's. Smaller than the Taylor's Dunlite, this handmade unit is the pride and joy of self-taught wind power enthusiast Jerry Forcier. Typical of the growing fraternity of backyard innovators in this exciting field, Jerry has devoted much of the past 12 months to studying wind mechanics and putting together a unit which incorporates what he believes to be significant improvements over existing equipment.

"Inefficient!" is what Jerry says of many of the design characteristics of currently available wind generators. With his eye on thrift and economy of operation, efficiency is the key. The demand for it goes from first catching the wind to the nature of the final product. His propeller is like others in number of blades (3) and in its automatic feathering device to protect the generator from too-high rpm's in heavy winds. Jerry's blades are custom designed, however, to meet the lighter-than-usual local wind conditions. He's made them almost twice as wide, about 14 inches, as common blades for better wind catching in light airs.

A major departure of his model is the direct-drive feature, eliminating the common step-up gear box. "It takes a lot of the wind's energy just to run gears; maybe as much as one-fourth of the energy caught by the prop is eaten up by gears. True, they make the generator turn faster for more output, but greatly reduce its effective life. With direct drive the slower-turning generator's life is extended three- to five-fold." There is a drop in output at lower rpm's, but Jerry feels he has increased output efficiency of this unit with special rewinding of the rotor (which turns inside the stator). By adding many pounds of copper wire to the rotor, he has partially offset the output drop of his lower rpm generator. Avoiding the gears also means less maintenance, fewer trips up the tower.

"I think I've got about a 3-3.5 kw generator here," says the inventor— certainly enough to power the household's lights, appliances (minus cooking and heating), and tools, given adequate wind.

"The electricity from it will be used in the form of Direct Current without inverting to AC. Producing DC just takes a lot less raw energy than is needed for AC production." We all live with AC, but except for televisions and stereos and a few other unadaptable items, DC power could do it all.

Jerry Forcier's wind-work and that of others across the country is answering a growing demand for decentralization and self-sufficiency in power production. People are fast becoming more energy-conscious as the limits of mass-produced energy from nonrenewable natural resources become apparent.

Jerry Forcier and his first model wind generator. Perpendicular to the propeller is the braking device that protects the generator in high winds.

Sources of Wind Power Equipment

Energy Alternatives
Box 223
Leverett, Mass.   01054

Zephyr Wind Dynamo Company
Box 241
Brunswick, Maine   04011

Scencenbaugh Electric, Inc.
P. O. Box 11174
Palo Alto, Calif.   94306
Plans for wind plants

Windworks
Box 329, Rte. #3
Mukwonago, Wisc.   53149
Plans for wind plants

Earthmind
26510 Josel Dr.
Saugus, Calif.   91350
Plans for wind plants

North Wind Power Company
Warren, Vermont   05674
New wind driven electric systems
Rebuilt wind electric plants
Plans for wind plants

Environmental Energies, Inc.
21243 Grand River
Detroit, Mich.   48219
New wind driven electric systems
Rebuilt wind electric plants

Independent Power Developers
Box 618
Noxon, Montana   59853
New wind driven electric systems

Real Gas and Electric Co.
P. O. Box "A"
Guerneville, Calif.   95446
New wind driven electric systems

111

Further Reading on Wind Power

Wind and Windspinners. Michael Hackleman and David House. Peace Press, Culver City, Calif. $7.50. Strong on "how-to" basics of building your own wind plant. Includes complete plans for a Savonius rotor wind system.

Electric Power from the Wind. Henry Clews. Solar Wind, Pubs., East Holden, Maine. $2. In the beginning (of the wind power renaissance; that is) there was Henry Clews. In this important booklet, Henry talks about why and how he got started with wind and makes some of the subject's more complicated concepts easy for the layman to understand.

Producing Your Own Power. Carol Stoner. Rodale Press, Emmaus, Pa. $8.95. Balanced, realistic overviews of the most promising alternative energy systems' experimenters and authorities on wind, solar, methane and wood power. Wind power is covered by Henry Clews and Jim De Korne, who describe some of the limitations and obstacles to homemade windmills.

Alternative Sources of Energy. Back Issues Book #1, edited by Sandy Eccli. $6.95. ASE, Milaca, Minn. For the past three years *Alternative Sources of Energy* has featured many "nuts and bolts" articles on owner-built wind power, always emphasizing innovation and reader-experimenter feedback. For where they've come from, see this anthology; for where they're going, subscribe to ASE at Rte. 2, Milaca, Minn. 56353 ($5 for six issues).

Energy Primer. Portola Institute, Menlo Park, Calif. $4.50. An outstanding source book on renewable forms of energy—solar, water, wind and biofuels. Detailed, up-to-date investigations of decentralized, small scale systems that serve the needs of the individual or small group. Wind section includes several original articles, along with comprehensive list of people and groups researching the subject. Also guide to presently available wind hardware.

Joe Carter

Treadle Power in the Workshop

With motor-driven power tools, one can work quickly and with little physical exertion. Many craftspeople feel that without them, they could not compete in the marketplace. Despite their advantages, however, I prefer not to use power tools. I find their noise and insistent high speeds unsettling and antithetical to the tranquil frame of mind I seek while working with wood. Although I am not yet skillful or patient enough to dispense with power tools altogether, it is my goal to have a completely "people-powered" woodworking shop.

My first step in this direction was to convert an old band saw to treadle power. In my design, the treadle turns a massive flywheel, which, in turn, drives the band saw. I operate the machine with one foot on the floor and the other pumping the treadle. As wide as the treadle is, I can stand directly in front of the blade or off to either side and still be able to pump. This feature is useful when cutting a long or large workpiece. A wide treadle is in this case more versatile than bicycle-type pedals, which confine the operator to one spot. However, by using both legs, as with pedals, one could probably generate more power than with only one leg. In my design, power is applied to the treadle only on the downstroke. The heavy counter-weighted flywheel evens out this periodic force and keeps the saw running at a steady pace.

Handmade Toys

Band saws are designed for making curved or scroll cuts. I have used mine extensively to make wooden toys from one-half inch and thinner stock. This kind of light work is very easy and pleasant. Also, I routinely step up to my band saw to make straight cuts in boards that one would ordinarily cut with a handsaw. I can definitely cut quicker and with less effort using leg muscles instead of arm muscles.

I appreciate having direct control over blade velocity. I can speed up for more power when cutting tough material, and slow down for intricate designs that require concentration. This is an advantage over motor-driven band saws that require you to stop and adjust the pulley ratio in order to change speeds.

My machine is capable of handling some very thick wood. The primary limiting factor is the strength of the operator. I've made chair rockers out of 1½-inch black walnut and brackets out of four-by-four-inch western red cedar, but these jobs leave me exhausted. The flywheel is definitely a help when cutting heavy stock.

The treadle turns a massive flywheel, which in turn operates the bandsaw.

With a band saw, one can turn abundant native materials into salable items. Small tree branches can be sliced into interesting buttons. They are finished by drilling two holes and sanding. Black walnut slices likewise are popular with handicrafters, so popular in fact that plastic imitations are on the market. As you slice up walnuts, you will also be accumulating a pile of sliced nutmeats, just the right size for cake or cookie recipes.

The base of this machine is three feet square, considerably larger than a comparable motor-driven tool. It needs to be this large to accommodate the flywheel and to provide stability despite the reciprocal action of the treadle.

I believe that there is more of the essence of a craftperson in his work if the energy that went into it comes from his own body. I identify more with things I have made with my own energy than with things made with the help of electricity. Operating a band saw can be hard work, but it is a good way to exercise while working indoors, and a productive way of keeping warm in the winter.

Construction

This design was worked out with an eye toward using the materials I already had on hand. Everything, except for some of the bolts, was second hand or salvage. Probably not many readers will have an old band saw to start with, but the treadle power-base could be adapted to any other tool with a similarly positioned pulley.

A number of companies sell kits and parts for making your own pulley-driven tools. (Two are: Gilliom Manufacturing Co., 1109 N. 2nd Street, St. Charles, Mo. 63301; and American Machine and Tool, Royersford, Pa. 14468.) While I have no personal experience with their products, they do seem to offer the do-it-yourselfer a way to put together his or her own tools at a savings. In some cases they offer two versions of a kit; if the more expensive one has better bearings, by all means choose it. One thing I learned early is the importance of good, low-friction bearings. Whatever friction there is in the machine will detract from the amount of your energy that is actually delivered to the workpiece.

The flywheel in my machine is from an old (late 1950's) Bendix front-loading home washing machine. The part that I used was a lens-shaped object about two feet in diameter that was actually stationary in its original application. The front of it served as the back wall of the washing chamber. It has a shaft, mounted on bearings, through the center of it. This shaft had the perforated washing basket on its front flange. The rear, threaded end of the shaft now passes through the wooden crosspiece of the treadle-base, and is anchored firmly in place by the nut that originally held the pulley. Thus the shaft is now stationary with the flywheel rotating on it; whereas originally the flywheel was a stationary base, with the shaft rotating in it. I think it is remarkable how a junked washer, relic of an opulent age, yielded up parts for a new tool in the post-industrial renaissance.

Mark Blossom

Rear Wheel Bicycle Adapter: Building Instructions

This design adapts any ordinary bicycle to a rear-wheel power takeoff to harness the power-of-the-pedal. For less than $45, you can build this simple mounting frame to use your bicycle one minute for grinding grain and the next minute to ride to the store.

Except for a welding or an acetylene outfit, tools needed to build this unit are commonly found around any workshop—drill, hacksaw, file, allen and common wrenches. Let your imagination improve on our design to best fit your specific needs and available materials.

Construction of the frame is the first step. Using 1¼-inch angle iron, build a floor frame 40 inches long and five inches wide. The rear spacing brace should be 7½ inches long to lap outside the frame to support two 18-inch uprights. Before welding, drill ten ¼-inch holes through the sides of the 40-inch pieces at one-inch intervals starting seven inches from the front end. *Caution:* Everything must be aligned symmetrically in this model for parallel positioning. Make sure the holes are aligned directly across from their mates. The bike frame mounts will bolt through these holes, and can be adjusted to fit different-sized bicycles.

To build each bicycle frame mount you will need a 14-inch upright, an eight-inch securing bar with ¼-inch holes drilled one inch from either end for bolting the mount to the 40-inch floor frame, a seven-inch balancing extension and a specially constructed frame-rest. Weld the three lengths of angle iron at right angles to each other.

The frame-rest is made from one-inch length of angle iron welded to a 1½x2-inch steel plate so that a ledge is formed for the bicycle frame to rest upon. A bolt fastens it to the upright. Another bolt fastens a ten-inch turnbuckle to the side of the upright. The turnbuckle should remain loose so you can swing it into place on the bike's frame before tightening.

The power arm is an 18-inch-long, five-inch-wide frame, hinged slightly rear of center on the frame's rear uprights via an axle and pillow blocks. Using 1¼-inch angle iron, space the two 18-inch lengths at the middle rear with five-inch lengths. Secure a set of sleeve bearing pillow blocks at the front end of the power arm in slots rather than holes, so the front pillow blocks are left adjustable. Center a second set slightly rear of center on the power arm and a third at the top of the frame's rear uprights.

Next you will need two axles to fit the pillow blocks. Thread the end of one with a right-handed thread to fit the Jacob's chuck. Flush with the other end, weld a 12-tooth sprocket and a 54-tooth sprocket separated ⅜ of an inch by washers. Place the axle through the pillow blocks, threaded end first, and attach the chuck. The other axle should have the remaining sprockets welded in inverse order to those on the first axle. Placing a six-inch wheel between the pillow blocks, insert the axle through the pillow blocks, wheel and bushings to secure the wheel. If the pillow blocks do not have lodging screws, you will need to secure the two axles with one more bushing on the outside of each pillow block.

For the finishing touches, adjust a chain to fit the sprockets. You can loosen the left pillow block and loosen the chain to change gears. Next, drill holes and attach a heavy duty spring between the rear end of the floor frame. This will keep the wheel on the power arm firmly wedged against the rear bicycle wheel.

To use your new power adapter, push the power arm to the floor (expanding the spring) and back your bicycle onto the frame. Lift the bicycle so that the rear wheel is off the ground, and set the frame on the two frame-rests. Swing the turnbuckles around to secure the frame in place and tighten. Let the power arm up and align it against the wheel. Fix your tool in the chuck, secure it to the table or wedge it against the floor. Most jobs will require two people for this setup—one to pedal, the other to operate and feed the implement being powered.

The power adapter is in position, and the rear wheel of the bicycle is in place on the two frame rests.

When building the rear wheel power takeoff, make sure the holes are aligned exactly across from their mates.

A Pedaled Lawn Mower

The power lawn mower, because it produces a good bit of noise and encourages us to sit, appears to be a likely candidate for retirement. Might there be a pedal replacement for the power mower?

Some years ago, Michael Shakespeare, an undergraduate at the Massachusetts Institute of Technology, wrote a thesis on the design of a lawn mower which would be pedaled rather than pushed. He turned out to be a superb designer and craftsman, and he produced a machine which was good-looking and practical. Besides a three-speed transmission, it had a differential drive to the wheels with a transmission brake; and by squeezing a handlebar lever and then pulling back on the handlebars, the whole cutting assembly could be lifted off the ground when traversing paths and the like.

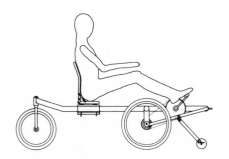

One design for a pedaled mower has a sliding seat and front-wheel drive. Its overall length will be seven feet.

The mower suffered from two drawbacks. One was the great weight of old cast-iron secondhand components which we had of necessity to buy. The second was the feet-high seating position. We had not yet learned that a few degrees in pedaling comfort and power output makes considerable difference.

In the interest of making the pedal lawn mower a reality, Rodale Press has funded another MIT student, Lee Laiterman, to pursue the subject further. After some preliminary study, Laiterman has arrived at the following specifications for his prototype lawn mower:

Wheelbase—45 inches; front track—35 inches; seat height—19 inches above ground; wheel—two- to 20-inch diameter in front, one- to 16-inch diameter in rear; cutter length—39 inches; front wheel drive—differential unit mounted on front axle; steering—rear wheel; overall length—seven feet.

The seat mount will be able to slide along the body, thus enabling adjustment for different-size riders. The cutting assembly is experimental. If it works, it will cut like an electric hedgetrimmer.

An eyebolt is included on the front end to facilitate storage on the wall. The seat back has an adjustment tilt for comfort. It can swing all the way down to facilitate wall storage. The seat is constructed of nylon webbing over a tubing skeleton.

Lee Laiterman plans to build a pedal mower, testing some of his theories. And, hopefully, other inventors and tinkerers will work on devising an efficient, lightweight pedal mower, thereby sending the power mower into retirement.

David Gordon Wilson

Irrigation Pumps

Present irrigation pumps employed in developing countries and powered by human muscle generally use the arms and back in swinging motions. There are a few examples of the leg muscles being used, particularly in Asia. Some different modern designs for foot-powered pumps suitable for local manufacture are an Archimedian screw driven from a bicycle frame with standard pedals; an endless-chain high-lift pump designed by Volunteers for International Technical Assistance (V.I.T.A.), with the chain going over the untired rear wheel; the rocking-pedal diaphragm pump designed by the International Rice Research Institute in the Philippines.

All of these are improvements over hand pumps, but none use the leg muscle optimally. Nor do the pumping devices have the highest hydraulic efficiencies available for the duty.

For low heads, centrifugal and axial-flow pumps are the most efficient. I once designed and made for V.I.T.A. an axial-flow hydraulic pump which was driven by the rear wheel of my bicycle when the wheel nuts rested in the stand. It was easy to pump between 100 and 200 gallons per minute over a few feet of head, far more than achievable by other pumps. But the drive was far from satisfactory, and the control

This foot-powered pump employs an Archimedian screw driven from the bicycle frame with standard pedals.

system which was needed to cope with different heads and different power inputs simultaneously was not solved. Here is an area which would reward good design.

David Gordon Wilson

Water Pumping

Water pumping is a basic energy user on the farm. Many house water systems use shallow well pumps. Many farms or rural locations have perfectly usable pitcher hand pumps. This unit will pump water with little effort if it is properly set up. An actuator rod from the

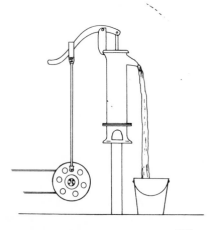

An actuating rod connected to the pump handle can supply the up-and-down motion to pump water. It will be possible to supply more water with less effort with foot power.

reciprocating output of the prime-mover (power source) can supply the up-and-down motion to pump water. Because the legs are stronger than the arms, it will be possible to pump more water in considerably less time with less effort than before.

Force-type pumps which resemble a pitcher pump are available, too. A force pump not only lifts water from the well, but also supplies it at pressure so it may be pumped to a storage tank, into a home or barn attic or loft. A force pump system might be useful for washing animals or farm machinery.

John McGeorge

Homemade Handles from Scratch

Hand-hewn handles replaced at home can be just as functional and more pleasing to the eye than commercial models. Most factory handles can be improved on, especially in the way they fit the individual hand. To make your own handles, you should have access to a workbench and wooden vise. You'll also need a basic set of tools— hand ax, saw, rasp-file, mallet and chisel, pocketknife, drawknife and sandpaper.

Wood for handles should be selected for soundness and natural shape. A straight branch from a solid hardwood, preferably hickory, is best.

1. Using either an existing handle or just personal preference, decide how long you want the handle to be and cut the limb accordingly.
2. Hew away excess wood on four sides with a hand ax while resting limb on a chopping block. Repeat until you've removed most, but not all, of the excess wood. Don't remove too much, or you won't be able to get a tight fit on the handle.
3. Switch to drawknife, pocketknife and rasp for further shaping. The shape may not get "right" for some time; it helps to stop and view the work from a distance or even leave it alone overnight. Test it for feel by swinging handle to simulate the way it will be used.

    Also, while using a drawknife on wood held in a workbench vise, take care not to rip out huge splinters. Develop a feel for

Driving in a wooden wedge will secure the axe head to the handle.

Fine shaping with drawknife and rasp follows hewing with a hand axe. Patience is the key here, as you'll spoil the chance to get a perfect grip by shaving off even the slightest bit too much.

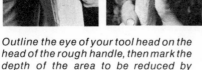

Outline the eye of your tool head on the head of the rough handle, then mark the depth of the area to be reduced by holding the head against the handle.

When the top of the handle has received its final shaping, secure it in the vise and make a sawcut down the middle, almost to the bottom of the tapered part.

Wedge should be thin and well tapered to avoid having the handle split below the head. Tap wedge in evenly until perfectly flush.

the grain, and if a splinter starts, turn the work in the vise and shave it off from the other direction.

4. With a pencil, mark the end to receive the head. Outline the eye (socket) of your ax or hammer on the end of the rough handle. Also hold the head against the handle so the tops of both are flush, and mark the depth of the area to be reduced. Work on the end with pocketknife and rasp-file, trimming the first inch or so until it fits well in the head. Don't jamb the tool head on the handle! Work the rest down to the same dimensions, taking into consideration any variations in the inner surfaces of the "eye" or socket of the tool. Now the handle can be filed and sanded to a rough finish.

5. To make the wedge that secures the tool head to the handle, use a piece of wood sawed from the end of the original tree limb. Saw off a section approximately one-half the depth of the tool-head socket. Using a mallet and a broad chisel, split a slice about $3/16$-inch thick from the center of this round section. Create a wedge by tapering from one end with a knife and chisel. Find the center line along the end of the handle and mark it.
6. Hold the handle in the vise and saw a vertical cut almost to the bottom of the tapered part.
   Pound the tool head on the handle (a few more fittings and shavings may be necessary). Then line up the wedge in the saw slot and tap it in evenly until it is perfectly flush. A small chunk of wood between the wedge and the mallet helps seat the wedge nicely.
7. All that remains is to give the handle a fine sanding to remove splinters, and apply some boiled linseed oil rubbed in well to bring out the grain and lubricate the wood. Any loosening of the head due to excessive dry heat can be remedied by soaking the end in water overnight.

The OGF All-Solar Greenhouse

Bob Hofstetter, head gardener at the New Organic Gardening Experimental Farm, was shaking his head, frankly skeptical. "We've already got a fine greenhouse for starting our plants. Sure, I'll use this one. But with only one wall clear, those plants are going to stretch right up to get the sun and fall over. Then it's going to get too cold at night. I just don't know—with no heat?"

Bob's heart was with the Research & Development project. He knew only too well how much it cost to heat the full-sized glass house at the Old Farm through the winter. But it produced plants faithfully.

Nearly anyone who has ever tried to keep vegetables growing into winter would have wondered about this one, too. When the sun's rays get short in December and January, and its light is barely strong enough to support growth—well, you need all the light you can get. And heat is another essential—an expensive one that keeps people from greenhouse gardening more than anything else. But the new greenhouse had only the clear front wall for a heat source.

This solar structure didn't look like it could provide those essentials. It's shaped like a shed with a long, steeply sloped front wall facing directly south. It's easy to picture the plants having to reach up for light. But they didn't. In fact, Bob now says he's fallen in love with the solar greenhouse: "All the plants had absolutely perfect color and shape." How is that possible when only ¼ of the total surface area lets in light?

The reason is so simple you wonder why greenhouse makers didn't think to use it sooner. Dr. Dave McKinnon, a physicist working with the Museum of Northern Arizona and the Atmospheric Sciences Research Center (of State University of New York at Albany), designed the Research & Development greenhouse. He explains it like this:

"In winter the sun rises and sets fairly far south on the horizon. That's why we have so little light to work with. But it's also why clear sidewalls wouldn't give us much extra light. By the time the sun is strong enough for plant growth—9:00 A.M. to 3:00 P.M. in dead winter— it's high enough to shine right in that clear front wall. The only light the design cuts out is indirect, like under a shade tree. Even if the other ¾ of the surface area were clear, the greenhouse would gain only ⅓ more light. But this way we can insulate the rest."

The time was right to sort through the wealth of information on solar collecting and heating, and apply it to greenhouses. Dave was convinced that greenhouses could be designed for more temperate climates which would operate on the sun's energy alone. This is an exciting idea for home vegetable production. And he explained some other things—like how much solar energy could be expected inside the greenhouse and what savings insulation would achieve—we came to share this conviction.

For almost everyone, fresh greens in winter are available only at tremendous transportation expenses, and their freshness is often questionable. With the cost of heating a small conventional greenhouse at least $300 a season, Dave's model would pay for itself on the fuel savings alone (not to mention the food) in just a few winters. We decided to work together and see how well it could be done.

That's how the 16-by-16-foot saltbox structure—a lot like a giant cold frame—came to stand completed at the New Farm in October of 1975. Right away, devices were installed to record daily maximum and minimum temperatures outside and inside, as well as the amount of solar energy entering the greenhouse. And just that fast, the energy efficiency of the structure began to prove itself.

For the initial testing period we didn't put any plants in. There were too many other things we wanted to watch. For the novices to solar technology among us, feeling the temperatures soar into the high eighties—sometimes the nineties—on any bright November morning was a rapid lesson in sun power. When a few of the nights dipped below freezing, the air inside the greenhouse held at 50 degrees, fine for most vegetable plants.

The design of the greenhouse was letting in almost all useful light. And just a month before its annual low point, the sun was delivering more than enough heat to warm the daytime air to the 70 degrees ideal for plant growth. The relatively warm nighttime temperatures inside showed that the solar greenhouse was capable of holding a lot of the energy in.

McKinnon had come east for a while to watch this greenhouse reacting to changing weather conditions. It also gave him a chance to work on techniques for improving its efficiency. He explained that being able to insulate ¾ of the building was the key to maintaining such warmth. The walls and roof all held 7½ inches of cellulose fiber insulation. For an idea of what that can do, imagine a long night of 20 degrees outside, but 50 degrees inside. The combined insulated wall space of this greenhouse was losing only ½ an energy unit (1 unit = 1,000 Btu's) each hour. By contrast, the ¼ of the surface area which is clear was passing nearly 6 energy units an hour.

Making the greenhouse air-tight is the first step to heat efficiency. But when the weather turns warm, two movable bottom panels and vents near the peak make it easy to cool. Inside, all joints are caulked to eliminate drafts. Polyethylene panels blanket the inner face at nightfall and in cloudy weather.

One of the first things Dave worked on was a way to cut those heat losses through the clear face of the greenhouse. We were using Kalwall Sunlite, a very clear fiberglass reinforced plastic. It has about the same good qualities for a greenhouse covering as glass does, including the ability to hold in heat rays. A layer of polyethylene, on the other hand, lets heat out extremely fast. But Dave found a way to use polyethylene as a supplement to the transparent wall. By wrapping wooden frames with it he built clear removable panels to fit behind the Kalwall on the rafters. They were light and inexpensive.

The sandwiches of air space they created made a big difference. One set of panels installed behind the clear wall cut its heat losses in half while retaining most of its transparency. Two sets of the panels cut losses down to just 1.4 energy units per hour with 30 degrees separating inside and outside temperatures.

The best part of this tactic is the way the transparent face now can be matched to the weather. On a clear, cold morning, the panels can be taken down to charge up the house. But when it's cloudy, they help the greenhouse coast through to fairer weather on its reserve heat. That option put us in control of a greater share of the energy that the greenhouse was absorbing.

McKinnon was really pleased that a self-sustaining, sun-heated greenhouse was getting much closer. He explained how he envisioned its possibility: "On a good day, the sun is placing about 150 energy units inside the house, and only a half of one unit all day is spent heating the inside air up to the 70 degrees we want. With our low heat losses at night now, there is a mountain of energy leftover. If we hoard it like misers, this greenhouse will run with almost zero outside energy."

What can happen to the extra energy? All of it eventually is used up balancing steady heat losses. Our greenhouse was taking in so much energy that it was often too hot inside to grow healthy plants. Potentially, though, all the surplus could be stored. The problem was that plants must cover most of the sunlit areas, so the storage material can't get much energy directly. Finding various ways around this dilemma absorbed a lot of our effort and continues to do so.

Especially in cloudy winters like ours, every bit of heat sooner or later becomes valuable to tide the little world in the greenhouse over a series of dim days. Ours had a built-in reservoir. Whenever it stayed 25 degrees warmer than the night air, all that heat was radiating from 2 feet of sun-warmed earth in the floor. No matter how cold the night, this reliable holdover from a bright day revealed itself on the morning temperature chart. There were cold, rainy spells, however, when plants in the house needed more.

The greenhouse lost virtually no heat through the ground. Dave had pointed out that even though the earth—as in a sun pit—moderates the temperature, it is relatively cool and will steadily drain off a lot of heat. So sheets of 2-inch plastic foam lined the foundation.

Still, not enough energy was going into storage; the too-high daytime temperatures we got regularly were a certain sign. Though the earth floor had the same storage capacity as 2,000 gallons of water, it was taking in heat very slowly. This was useful over a long term, but to moderate daily temperatures the greenhouse needed added storage.

Through late January and February, we gathered metal containers, painted them black, and stacked them against the back wall. They were filled with water, which would absorb the heat much faster than earth. And positioning them high put them in closer contact with the heat in the air. We are quite sure that this will help capture more of the available heat, even though the black containers don't receive much direct radiation.

A few inventive people have already benefited from a slightly different approach to the knotty problem of heat storage. They vent it off, but into their homes! Any greenhouse is, after all, a large solar collector. In March, 1976, OGF reported on Christopher Fried's solar greenhouse, which actually uses ⅔ of its solar face directly as a hot-air collector. Bill Yanda of the Solar Sustenance Project in New Mexico has built several attached structures which function primarily as winter vegetable plots. All excess heat flows into the home through a window or doorway. The beauty of this system is its simplicity; there's no need to remove heat from the air. And at night the home feeds heat back to the greenhouse.

Yet another possibility, especially when the greenhouse can't be attached to the home's south wall, is to use an outside heat source. Bill and Marsha Mackie of Oregon have attached a small flat plate collector to one side of their solar greenhouse. This way they can tap into direct radiation without sacrificing space inside. The hot water is stored along the back wall in a large tank which also grows fish.

A freestanding solar greenhouse in cold climates will likely need some auxiliary system like this to boost the crops past the occasional frigid and cloudy stretches. With our water-storage system in its infancy, we installed a small heater (something we don't plan to rely on) just to keep temperatures above freezing. We dearly wanted to see how well vegetables would grow in our light quality.

Bob Hofstetter gave rave reviews. Everyone was surprised when he claimed superior plant growth in the solar greenhouse. Now he feels that constant warm temperatures encourage weak, spindly growth— and that the cool nights held insect pests in check. The solar greenhouse produced excellent lettuce, excellent chard, and even some early spring tomatoes!

When Dave McKinnon returned to Arizona, he immediately built some modifications into a sister greenhouse. One interesting feature is a steeply sloped rear wall. Painted white on the inside, it should reflect substantially more light to the plants. The main goal of Research and Development's work will be to develop improved ways of getting excess heat out of the air and into storage. Hopefully, when the details have been worked out, we'll have a greenhouse that practically runs itself for free, year after year.